Windows of Light

Shining

With Love

By

Patricia Ann Farnsworth-Simpson.

شد♣شد🏛شد♣ششـد

Published by
Passion for Poetry Publishers.

IBSN   978-0-6151-9123-2

شـ♣شـ♣شـ🕌شـ♣شش

Foreword

Born in Derbyshire, England the daughter of a coalminer,
Pat was raised the only girl with six brothers. She was a widowed
mother by her 18th birthday, then later married a childhood school
friend Tony. Now married 48yrs they have three children, and a large
family of grandchildren and great grandchildren. For 18yrs before
retirement they ran a family
Hotel in Scarborough UK. Where Pat became a spiritual healer and
healing tutor for her local church, this is where she first got her
inspirations for writing poetry.
Pat overwhelmed with fear and anxiety because one of her children
was seriously ill, found that keeping her mind occupied this way,
writing about her thoughts helped her through the worry, she also
gained the deep sense of calm needed at the time to be strong for her
child. Pat believed prayer helped very much in her child's recovery and
that all the poetic words she has written were truly inspired......
Admitting to having no great education Pat says,
"I myself am both delighted and surprised to see my poetic thoughts
in print, each phrase I know was given to me to help me through a
very tough time in life, now I believe they are given to me to help and
guide others along the pathway of life to find love, understanding and
GOD.
This is a poetry book to show love of God, love of family and love of
life, full of inspired poems given to Pat by her Spiritual Guiding
Teachers above. It is a book written to let God's light shine through in
her words to give much joy to Christians and hopefully inspire other's
to see The Light!
The Light of God above that shines down always to guide and protect
us... so that one day we will be light enough with love in our Soul to
rise to Heaven above ...

If you're in pain..........There are words to help heal!
If you feel lost............There are words to guide!
If you are sad.............Let these words bring joy!
If you feel remorse.....Let these words wash it away!
If you have faith.........These words will inspire!
If you feel love...........These words you will adore!

God Bless! I pray you enjoy

Pat Simpson
xxx

3

Page One Table of Contents

*^♠♟♠^**^♠♟♠^***^♠♟♠^*

شد♣شد♣شد🏠شد♣ششد

Page Two Table of Contents

*^♠🏠♠^**^♠🏠♠^**^♠🏠♠^*

Page Three Table of Contents

*^♠♟♠^**^♠♟♠^**^♠♟♠^*

Acknowledgements

With thanks to God and His healing Angels!
To loved ones gone before who come in close to inspire!
To my loving Husband Tony that truly is my rock!
To our children who have brought joy and made life complete!
They're our future God Bless them each and everyone!

*^♠🏛♠^**^♠🏛♠^**^♠🏛♠^*

LORD BLESS US ALL

With your loving light
Let it touch all within your sight!

*^♣🏠♣^**^♣🏠♣^**^♣🏠♣^*

Windows of Light

Windows of light kept shining bright,
Built to let in God's Heavenly light,
Created with beautiful pictures seen,
To honor God's love that's evergreen!

*^♠⇧♠^*

Windows let light come shining through,
Walls of darkness both old and new,
Darkness that can hide heartache and sin,
Hurt and pain so you crumble within!

*^♠⇧♠^*

A slight crack is all we need to see,
God's shining light beaming constantly!
A little hope is what's needed to do the trick,
Of penetrating darkness built up thick.

*^♠⇧♠^*

شد❖شد🏛شد❖ششد

Yes! A hole in the wall will let God's light,
Come shining through with strength so bright!
Even if bricked up through pain and shame,
God's light will shine on us, just the same!

*^♠🏛♠^*

So if you build up a wall then open your mind,
Look for the window God gives to find,
A window so precious to let in the light,
To take away darkness and also fright!

*^♠🏛♠^*

If you can't see a window, chop out a hole,
Let in God's light that the darkness stole,
Light is love it is healing too,
So look for ways to let it shine on you!

*^♠🏛♠^*

Let your eyes be the windows of your soul,
To keep them open, when shut, that is the goal!
Of seeing God's light shining in and out you,
To fill you with love your whole life through!

*^♠🏛♠^**^♠🏛♠^**^♠🏛♠^*

Thank Thee Lord

For the gift of faith and peace within,
WE THANK THEE LORD!

*^♠⬆♠^*

For the forgiveness of sin
WE THANK THEE LORD!

*^♠⬆♠^*

For the home of Heaven up above,
WE THANK THEE LORD!

*^♠⬆♠^*

For unconditional everlasting love,
WE THANK THEE LORD!

*^♠⬆♠^*

For the Planet Earth and all there-on,
WE THANK THEE LORD!

*^♠⬆♠^*

For the promise of life to be won!
WE THANK THEE LORD!

*^♠⬆♠^**^♠⬆♠^**^♠⬆♠^*

11

Windows of The Soul

Your eyes are the windows of your soul,
So keep them clean and bright,
Let them sparkle with the love,
Of all you see in sight!

*^♠⇧♠^*

Let them shine with love also,
For that which you can't see,
For all you feel that comes around,
Like air to nourish thee!

*^♠⇧♠^*

Be aware of all of your feelings,
For each one of them will show,
In the windows of your eyes,
Then all will see and know!

*^♠⇧♠^*

When the heart within you feels loved
Giving out love too will make them shine,
For they glitter clearly with happiness,
But go dull when the heart does pine!

*^♠⇧♠^*

So the best way to keep the windows
Of your soul shining bright,
When dull and Oh! So badly smeared
Is to polish them up right!

*^♠⇪♠^*

By looking out around you,
Yes! Looking out not looking in,
Showing other's with heartache too,
Compassion will help you win!

*^♠⇪♠^*

The loving light that is needed,
To put a sparkle in the windows there,
For you gain much by understanding,
And showing other's that you care!

*^♠⇪♠^*

One sure way of keeping the windows,
Of your Soul shining bright each day,
Is to let the loving light of God,
Come inside them to stay!

*^♠⇪♠^**^♠⇪♠^**^♠⇪♠^*

13

شـ๑شـ๑شـ๑شـ๑ششـ

'Springs Joy!

Welcome
All you pretty birds,
How lovely to see you again,
Winters gone,
Now our days are seen much warmer,
We are blessed to hear your song,
Springs Joy!

*^♠⭐♠^**^♠⭐♠^**^♠⭐♠^*

Summer Sun

Joyful
Summer days of fun,
Butterflies flutter, lavender,
Now is wealth
For bees active honey making,
Their sweet delicious preserve,
Good Health!

*^♠⭐♠^**^♠⭐♠^**^♠⭐♠^*

ش♣ش♣ش🏰ش♣ش♣ش

Golden Days

Golden
Colors now abound,
Leaves all fall and the birds gather,
To migrate,
Now the only singing is done
By the rustling of the leaves,
Swept clean!

*^♠🏰♠^**^♠🏰♠^**^♠🏰♠^*

Winter Magic!

Dark nights,
North winds blow, cold ice,
Snow settling for children to play,
Winters bed!
Now the lovely little Robin,
Really stands out with his breast,
Blood red!

*^♠🏰♠^**^♠🏰♠^**^♠🏰♠^*

Let Your Healing Light Shine

Dear God let your loving light shine down,
On all the people in my home town,
Let everyone around absorb it and see,
How good they feel with your love flowing free!

*^♠⇧♠^*

Then let them all glow with real good health,
To realize that this is Earth's true wealth,
Not the oil or gold that we see mined each day,
But love and well being inside us to stay!

*^♠⇧♠^*

Dear God as a Mother I ask this with heart true,
And I know all mother's ask the same thing too,
So let me represent them all please do,
When I speak my words in prayer to you!

*^♠⇧♠^*

Dear God! Let your healing light shine everywhere,
To heal the troubles and rifts that bring despair,
So that children everywhere can grow and be strong,
Within the family of man that they belong!

*^♠⇧♠^**^♠⇧♠^**^♠⇧♠^*

شـﺤشـﺤشـ🏠شـﺤششـﺤ

Blocked Light

Light it can penetrate the darkest black,
Only a solid wall stops it in its track,
Light will penetrate into caverns most deep,
Wherever there's an opening it will seep!

So remember when you are feeling low,
There is no depths the mind can go,
Where the light of love cannot be,
If you open up your heart for it to see!

*^♠🏛♠^*

Determinedly cover yourself with light,
If your chest is feeling hard and tight,
Because of walls you built with might,
Thinking they'd protect you right!

*^♠🏛♠^*

Walls round the heart are not a protection,
All they do is show total rejection,
Rejection of help when there's a need,
Rejection of any loving deed!

*^♠🏛♠^*

شد♣شد♣شد🏛️شد♣ششد

Walls like this don't protect or repair,
A heart that's broken needing care,
The only way a broken heart will heal,
Is by opening it up to let it feel!

*^♠🏛️♠^*

Love come flowing in shining bright,
From all who care to make you right,
Never reject any light of love,
Let it always settle on you like a dove!

Absorb it then through and through,
Till it's thoroughly inside of you,
Then it will flow out for others to see,
There are no walls blocking the light from thee!

*^♠🏛️♠^**^♠🏛️♠^**^♠🏛️♠^*

The Four Letter Word

There is one four letter word,
That is easy to pronounce,
It means a huge amount
Yet it doesn't weigh an ounce!
You can't hold it in your hands
But you can feel it all around,
You can't see it with your eyes,
But you know it can be found!
You always want to keep it,
Yet you're happy to give away,
It's such a joy to shower in it,
Each and every day!
It is always the same,
Yet it does vary so,
You can give it to a stranger,
And even things that grow!
You can see it, feel it, hold it,
Give it away and yet still keep,
For this four letter word,
We always want to reap!
So set the seeds and sow it,
Where ever you may go,
Then the four letter word
Will be yours to know!

*^♠♜♠^*

Light as a feather,
Open like a book,
Valued immensely,
Endless emotion!

Light to always flow,
Often to give away,
Very deep when good
Everlasting it should.

*^♠♜♠^**^♠♜♠^**^♠♜♠^*

Religion

The word I hate most of all today,
Is the word RELIGION.
Because all it seems to say to me,
Segregation and Division!

*^♠♟♠^*

How I wish and pray, that all mankind,.
Would, hit it on the head.
And do away with saying RELIGION,
By just saying LOVE instead!

*^♠♟♠^*

For if man is built in God's image,
Then He' must look, like you and me.
And if He' does look like you and me,
Then more than one color, we see!

*^♠♟♠^*

And if He is more than one color,
Then He's probably more than one name.
So why can't we all accept that;
The 'GOD' we 'LOVE' is the same.

*^♠♟♠^**^♠♟♠^**^♠♟♠^*

شد♣شد🏰شد♣شش

Going Somewhere

He's in a hurry going somewhere,
But nowhere is where he'll be,
If he keeps driving down the road,
Like he does so recklessly!

*^♠🏰♠^*

Making his brakes screech,
Around every bend he went,
Leaving rubber tyre marks,
With clouds of dust up sent!

*^♠🏰♠^*

He's in a hurry and not thinking,
What's out of sight round there,
Maybe a dog or child at play
Or a man in a wheelchair!

*^♠🏰♠^*

Then again how often do we hear?
A Mother with pram's been knocked down,
Whilst walking on the pavement,
Just going to the Town!

*^♠🏰♠^*

So his great hurry to get somewhere,
Might stop him and others who,
May end up getting somewhere,
Where they never wanted too!

*^♠🏰♠^**^♠🏰♠^**^♠🏰♠^*

شد♣شد🏛️شد♣شد

Unforgettable in 3 Styles

Acrostic:

Under no illusion
No false impression here
For you have truly given
Openly my Dear,
Reasons to remember
Greatly with love.
Everything about you
To keep in part,
Touching so tenderly
All of my heart.
Best memories ever
Lovingly now they have grown,
Everlasting to be, forever shown!

*^♠🏛️♠^*

Chain Poem:

Remember forever this one day,
Day spent in sunshine bright,
Bright and cheerful as I recall,
Recall how birds sang together all,
All that afternoon we strolled together,
Together hand in hand tightly held,
Held so that we we're just as one,
One who never wanted the day, done!
Done though as all days that turn to night,
Night like the day so unforgettable,
Unforgettable making memories livable!

*^♠🏛️♠^*

Senryu:

So happily held,
The memories that we call,
Unforgettable!

*^♠🏛️♠^**^♠🏛️♠^**^♠🏛️♠^*

شد♣شد🏯شد♣شد

Our Soul's Reap

As I swim in the sea everyday,
To the Lord above I do pray,
Asking for his water's blue,
To cleanse my body through and through!

*^♠🏯♠^*

To wash away all hurt and pain,
Then I ask for His healing to be sent again!
To family and loved one's across the sea!
For them to be healed just like me!

*^♠🏯♠^*

For them to feel joy and happiness each day,
With a healthy body and a heart at play!
Then has I swim below in the ocean deep,
I pray one day, God will our Souls reap!

*^♠🏯♠^**^♠🏯♠^**^♠🏯♠^*

شـ♣شـ🏛شـ♣شـشـ

The Sun and The Wind

The sun is shining the wind is blowing,
Making tree's shadows dance,
Shaking the leaves off their branches,
To give life alone a chance!

*^♠🏛♠^*

The sun is shining the wind is blowing,
Fanning any warmth in the sun,
The trees are forced to get undressed,
With leaf life now all done!

*^♠🏛♠^*

The sun is shining the wind is blowing,
Keeping the skies clear above,
The trees stand naked but proud,
Fighting to hold on to love!

*^♠🏛♠^*

The sun is shining the wind is blowing
Trees struggle with the cold,
Shorter days and longer nights,
Makes them feel so old!

*^♠🏰♠^*

The sun is shining the wind is blowing,
Getting less bitter each day,
Swirling softly around the trees,
So they gently bend in play!

*^♠🏰♠^*

The sun is shining the wind is blowing,
But gently now and warm,
The trees delighted relax to see,
New leaves begin to swarm!

*^♠🏰♠^*

The sun is shining the wind is blowing,
To give trees the best sight seen,
Of sunlight shining and dancing through,
Leaves now on trees so green!

*^♠🏰♠^**^♠🏰♠^**^♠🏰♠^*

My Lord's Love!

Your love Dear Lord is like fresh air,
To fill my lungs and heart, „
They then pump it around me,
Till I feel you in every part!

*^♠⇧♠^*

You're the shiver down my spine,
The electricity in my hair
The vibration in my fingertips,
Yes! I feel You everywhere.

*^♠⇧♠^*

Without Your love, I'd struggle to live,
Like breathing in bad stale air,
I'd pant and gasp the rest of my life,
Till interest was lost and didn't care!

*^♠⇧♠^*

Yes! That would be me without your love,
An empty shell, just void of life,
I wouldn't have any purpose left,
All I'd know is misery and strife.

*^♠⇧♠^*

But I Have' your love, and Lord I know
Just what you have done for me,
You lifted me from the darkest depths,
And You gave me dignity.

*^♠⇧♠^*

Yes! You' are the fresh air I need daily,
To fill me and make me glow,
With joyous, loving vitality,
That I pray will always grow!

*^♠🏠♠^*

Now I've found you, I can't live without you,
I need you completely inside of me,
For only your love gives me everything,
That I need for my heart to be free!

*^♠🏠♠^*

Yes! Your love Dear Lord fills me,
With a warmth that I can feel,
Changing negative vibes that destroy
Into loving positive ones to heal!

*^♠🏠♠^**^♠🏠♠^**^♠🏠♠^*

I Love Light

I love to see light shining on the sea so blue,
Sunlight, moonlight what ever shimmers through!

I love to see how a crystal comes alive with light,
To send wonderful rainbows into the room so bright!

I love the light in a tunnel how it shows the way,
The first streaks of sunlight at the break of day!

I love to see the light that comes with understanding,
The joyful light of love when it isn't demanding!

I love to see the light gently flickering through trees,
As leaves gently rustle and dance with the breeze!

I love the light of love that glows in each eye,
Of little children questioning," Why! Tell me why?"

I love the light of love that glows in Jesus's Face,
In the stained glass windows made to honour his grace!

I love knowing of the light that comes to show the way,
To our home up in Heaven at the end of the day!

There where I know the pure light will be shining above,
In each and every face of the people I Love!

Tony's Guided Meditation!

Tony couldn't sleep so I did a meditation to fill him with love,
Saying, "Breathe in that golden light that's shining above,
Every breath you breathe in you feel energized and lighter,
By exhaling all negative you're now golden and brighter"

Then guiding him into a meditation I said!

See yourself walking in a meadow, the grass is long,
Swaying in the breeze gently like music in a song!
Among the grass you see many flowers growing wild,
A most colorful sight to make you beguiled!

There just in front of you is a Rabbit with her young,
Chewing on the clover that's in this meadow sprung!
Because you're so light they don't know you're there,
So you can go up close like an Angel showing care!

*^♠♙♠^*

Then three mice come running out a hole to play,
A few sparrows too come near to peck at hay!
The rabbits, mice and birds aware of one another,
Play happy with no fear at all of each other!

*^♠♙♠^*

29

Then a Eagle hovering above makes the mice all run,
Into the hole and the sparrows they fly away, gone!
Mother Rabbit runs calling her babies to follow,
Quickly in the warren that's there in the hollow!

*^♠♔♠^*

All the rabbits get to safety except the last one,
When the Eagle swoops down thinking dinner, done!
All at once to save the rabbit you show yourself tall,
The rabbit runs faster and the Eagle is off an all!

*^♠♔♠^*

Happy you'd saved the rabbit and still feeling light,
You walk through the meadow to a stream in sight,
As the stream trickles fast over rocks in good flow,
You're reflection attracts you to a still part below!

*^♠♔♠^*

While looking at your face you see through it a trout,
Down still as if sleeping not swimming about,
You reach down and lovingly tickle its belly and back,
You pick it up to stroke it, then you put it back!

*^♠♔♠^*

Then you see a Frog on a lily pad laughing at you,
Saying, "Why didn't you eat it, he'd have been good for you!
You reply, "I'm golden and light and full of love for all,
When your Soul love's like mine, you don't need meat at all!

Then somehow the meditation started going wrong
When I said near the Frog a fly came buzzing along,
The Frog flicked out his tongue and swallowed him whole
Before you had chance to save his soul!

*^♠⬆♠^*

You look at the Frog thinking poor Fly,
Why did you eat him you wanted to cry!
But before you could Frog said "That's his end,
You see I'm not full of love like you my friend!"

*^♠⬆♠^*

At this the meditation it ended swiftly short,
As we both laughed at the Frog and fly getting caught!
But the meditation had worked in its way,
Because it made Tony relax at the end of the day!

*^♠⬆♠^**^♠⬆♠^**^♠⬆♠^*

Twice Wed

I had to get married twice, I tell you it is true,
But both times I was happy, never once was I blue!

Sixteen when first wed, pregnant but it wasn't shot gun,
I wed because I wanted to, that's why the deed was done!

My Dad said he'd care for me and the baby I carried,
Because you're pregnant you don't have to be married!

But I told him I loved Harold, that I was happy to be wed,
There was nothing I'd rather be, than wife and mother I said!

So the marriage took place, not a plush grand affair,
Just a simple registrar ceremony I was happy to share!

Happy was I being a wife, we got a house of our own quick,
I had my son, all was great, till Harold was taken sick!

*^♠♟♠^*

شد♣شد♣شد♠شد♣ششد

He died December the twelfth, to be buried on the day,
Before my 18th birthday, I was lost, with life swept away!

I moved back to Mam and Dad, later Dad said to my brother,
Take Pat out with you, she's still a young girl like any other!

So I went with Wilf and school pals, to the local dance,
That Tony Simpson was a good jiver, I did learn by chance!

When he asked me to dance, I really got a surprise to see,
That he had grown up so much, to be inches taller than me!

Yes! In the village dance hall, Tony could bop the best,
So it wasn't long before I danced, with him and not the rest!

Within the year we were strong, for he lived on the same row,
Calling for me and my baby son, who he loved dearly I know!

*^♠⇑♠^*

Yes! I had to get married again, but this wasn't shot gun too,
For my Mam and Dad both said, they'd support me through!

But wanting to wed I did, getting a house down same row,
Where we happily lived together, to watch our family grow!

So yes! I have been wed twice, pregnant both times too,
But I haven't been a floozy' that I can promise you!

I've only had two men in my life, Happily I wed them both,
But none was a shot gun wedding, And I kept vows and oath!

شد♣شد🏠شد♣ششد

Close the Door

Close a door to shut out wind and rain,
But you cannot shut it on hurt and pain,
Close a door on all you know is wrong,
If not it will always roll along!

*^♠🏠♠^*

Close a door to put an end to things,
So once again it's your heart that swings,
Not the door left swinging on the latch,
Hoping the wind changes to get the catch!

*^♠🏠♠^*

Close a door to let go of dead wood,
When you know its right that you should,
Love that's lost, you have to let go,
Even though it hurts and pains you so!

*^♠🏠♠^*

Close the door when you've found God above
To keep him inside you with his love,
When locked up deep chuck away the key,
For that is where He truly wants to be!

*^♠🏠♠^**^♠🏠♠^**^♠🏠♠^*

Forty-Eight Years

We've been married for forty-seven years,
We've had our heartaches and we've had tears,
But you've been strong and you've been true,
And that's the thing that's got me through!
Now I Thank God you're here today,
With me to celebrate your birthday!

HAPPY BIRTHDAY
´PAT´
All my Love
TONY xxx

Comment
Tony wrote this on my birthday card for my birthday
Which is the day before our wedding anniversary

*^♠⛫♠^*

TONY

You have always and ever been around,
To pick me up from off the ground,
I cannot remember any day,
When our paths didn't cross in any way!
With my brother Wilf being your best friend,
Many hours playing together we did spend!
Born in the same village down the same backs,
We ventured together down all of the tracks!
Playing in the meadow running down the vale,
Then later exploring many a Derbyshire Dale!
Now I pray to God and in every prayer,
I ask we'll have many more days to share,
That we will have the wonderful fate,
Of having a Diamond wedding to celebrate!
Knowing that if we get there both still together,
Like creaking gates, we'll last forever!

I LOVE YOU!

PAT xxx

To Forgive Not Judge

We come here to learn as we live
How not to judge but how to forgive
To master this trait we must try each day
Be it at home, work or out at play!

*^♠⛪♠^*

It seems early in life we know how to judge
Turn on each other and refuse to budge,
Mean enough to strip meat from the bone
And so often willing to cast first stone!

*^♠⛪♠^*

This is a task that we on Earth must fight,
Remembering always we're in Gods sight.
When we judge, we go against all he's taught,
For this isn't the bait he wants to see caught.

*^♠⛪♠^*

Do unto others as you'd have them do you,
That's the message we should follow through,
Though we do have to uphold the laws of man
In our heart and soul we should judgment ban.

*^♠⛪♠^*

God our Father is the only one who qualifies
To judge because of his all seeing eyes,
If sorry when wrong, then forgiveness he shows
Like his everlasting love that constantly flows.

*^♠⛪♠^*

ش♣ش♦ش🏠ش♣ششش

God's forgiven man for all he's done
Even the act of murdering his precious son,
So He doesn't ask more of you than He
Because how more forgiving can anyone be!

*^♠🏠♠^*

The act of forgiveness must start within
By forgiving yourself for each of your sin,
Love yourself and then forgive yourself too
For if you can't then don't expect others to!

*^♠🏠♠^*

Once true forgiveness as filled your heart,
The bitterness within it will all depart.
To leave you full of forgiving love,
And content for God be judge above.

Forgive
don't
Judge

*^♠🏠♠^**^♠🏠♠^**^♠🏠♠^*

ﺵﺵﺵﺵﺵﺵﺵ

Dear Lord Above

Dear Lord above I do pray,
On my knees to you this day,
For all the things I wish to say,
To ask of you in a simple way!

*^♠⇧♠^*

That all the people on Earth find,
Other people are also kind!
Give them aid to face daily grind,
For happiness and peace of mind,

*^♠⇧♠^*

Let all experience awakenment,
To help overcome bereavement,
Let forgiving overcome resentment,
Bless all with contentment!

*^♠⇧♠^*

This I ask of you Dear Lord!
So that peace will be restored,
For people to live in one accord!
With you in heart, their reward!

*^♠⇧♠^**^♠⇧♠^**^♠⇧♠^*

Both Sad & Glad

We all know about Heaven that it has life of worth,
But that don't stop the sadness when we lose one from Earth!
It doesn't take away the heartache, or the deep sense of loss,
That loved one's must have felt, when Jesus was on the cross!

*^♠⇑♠^*

The joy they must have felt, when he showed them life goes on,
Would have given them a lift, whilst still being sad He'd gone!
But knowing they are still living, doesn't really erase the pain,
Even though we all know one day we will meet them again!

*^♠⇑♠^*

Though loved ones go to Heaven where one day we hope to be,
Where we know they'll are waiting with joy for us to see!
It don't take away the pain of not seeing them with our eyes,
But yet when we do think of them, they feel close no surprise!

*^♠⇑♠^*

For they are deep inside us, etched by love into our heart,
Where we keep and cherish them, making them still a part!
Of the life we are still living, knowing just what they would say,
To any problem we may have, to help make it go away!

*^♠⇑♠^*

So though sad we cannot touch them with hands or with lips,
We're still so happy to find they're far closer than finger tips!
That's when we find it's possible, to be both happy and sad,
Heartbroken, lost, lonely, yet full of joy to feel lovingly Glad!

*^♠⇑♠^**^♠⇑♠^**^♠⇑♠^*

41

The Four Things Needed

There are only four things that will mend,
A once loving but now broken heart,
Though we know what these four things are,
It is hard to give them a working start!

It is because it's hard we suffer,
Believing them we'll never find,
But with number one TIME passing,
They then start to filter to mind!

The four things I know, you know!
But when hurting one can forget,
The four things that is needed,
To forget what you shouldn't forget!

What you shouldn't forget is, You Must Forget,
The pain that you're going through,
No.1.TIME passing helps the healing process,
So don't keep raking over the embers anew!

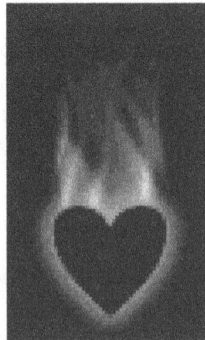

*^♠♛♠^*

ش‍ـش‍ـ♣‍ش‍ـ🏠‍ش‍ـش‍ـ♣‍ش‍ـش‍ـش‍ـ

You never cook with wood on a BBQ,
When it's red, burning with bright flame,
You have to let the ash settle on top,
Takes TIME but that's the secret of the game!

So if you think of your heart as the embers,
That's been painfully burning bright,
When the dust is starting to settle,
Don't go poking them up with might!

You'll never will really forget the pain,
That comes with losing I know,
But you must FORGET to stop reminding,
Yourself how much you hurt so!

So to FORGET poking pain is the second thing,
The third one is to FORGIVE,
God, fate, others and self,
For destroying the life you wanted to live!

The fourth thing is you must feed your heart,
Don't keep it cracked with an empty hole,
But fill it with LOVE once more,
For that's the only thing to make it whole!

Without love the heart is just a pump,
That feels heavy working inside,
There's only love that will lighten it,
To fill you soul with pride!

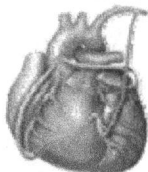

*^♠🏠♠^*

43

ﺷـﺶﺷـﺶﺷـﺶﺷﺶ

So never be scared of loving again,
And again and again if there's need,
For loving is the one thing,
You'll never be accused of having greed!

So if you find your heart is broken,
Practice these four things to get rid of pain,
Give yourself TIME, FORGET, FORGIVE,
And make LOVE fill your heart once again!

If you can't find LOVE like the one you've lost,
Then look around in another direction,
Love of God love of life love of everything,
Where you can show affection!

For it's only by giving and showing love,
That you will see it come back to you,
For the aura of a loving person attracts,
Others when, they see LOVE in you is true!

Concluding verse by Poet Pam Fuller aka seashells shoreline:

"So if you find your heart is broken,
Practice doing these four things now,
Give yourself TIME, FORGET and FORGIVE,
To make LOVE fill your heart somehow!

*^♠🏛♠^**^♠🏛♠^**^♠🏛♠^*

شش♣شد🏛شد♣ششد

Leaves & Trees

In Spring Mother Nature she does give,
A bursting of leaves to show trees live!
In Summer leaves frolic with the breeze,
On the beautiful green blooming trees!

*^♠🏛♠^*

The leaves then change to Yellow, Red, Gold,
In the fall they're lovely to behold!
But then as the season says they fall,
To rot as if never having lived at all!

*^♠🏛♠^*

With no leaves the trees are very bare,
Looking dead without even a shroud to wear!
Relying on roots that are very deep!
To face Winter as if in a dead sleep,

*^♠🏛♠^*

But cometh Spring once again we see,
Leaves budding again so generously!
Leaves have come and gone since life begun,
Let's Pray the cycle keeps moving on!

*^♠🏛♠^**^♠🏛♠^**^♠🏛♠^*

ﺷﺸﺷﺸﺷﺸﺷﺷ

Shining Love

Dear Father God in Heaven above,
Please let your shining light of love,
Shine down from Heaven on to me,
Till my body is filled completely!

Then let it swiftly through me flow,
To help the love in my heart grow,
Then let this love be pumped around,
Just like blood in my body found!

With every breath I take let the air be,
Full of your loving light to enter me,
Please let me receive this gift from above,
Till I inhale and exhale only love!

*^♠♙♠^*

ش♣شد🂱شد♣ششد

Then each breath I release please let it be,
Added to the light shining down from Thee!
So that my children and all I greet,
Take a share so they too, are complete!

In each word I speak let your love flow,
Into the ears of others to grow,
So that they too will be filled like me,
With pure shining love coming from Thee!

*^♠🂱♠^**^♠🂱♠^**^♠🂱♠^*

My Mother & Brother's Day

In Nineteen Hundred and Two,
Lady's had nothing to do,
Work they did flout as they just sat about
In Nineteen Hundred and Two!

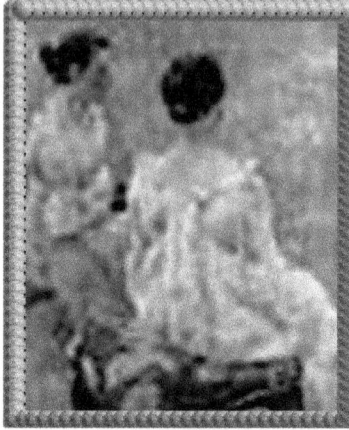

But this didn't apply to my Mother,
Born, November 14th 1902.
Being eldest girl in a big family,
She had to help her Mother all day through!
With no Bakers for bread in them days,
Or electric washing machine,
She scrubbed the floors on her knees,
Daily to keep them clean.
-

*^♠⏛♠^*

At 14 years she then went nursing,
Helping out wherever needed,
Through First World War then after
Her nursing it till succeeded!
Only stopping to have a family,
But then turned to nursing once more,
Recommended for therapy by the Doctor,
After the Grim reaper had been to the door!

*^♠⏛♠^*

ش♣ش♠ش♣شش

To take away her beloved son,
Born on her own birthday in thirty four,
But he got killed at fourteen down the pit,
So my Mother needed help then for sure!
So to get her out the house
To keep her mind and hands busy too,
With TB rife and nurses short,
My Mother did what she had to do!
By working nights at the hospital,
Caring for family and home all day through,
My Mother worked herself through the pain,
But I missed her so much I tell you!

*^♠♠♠^*

I still miss you today Mother Dear!
I miss my loving brother Ken too,
Today would have been your birthdays,
So I am feeling so close to you!
Mam! You'd now be one hundred and five,
Ken he will be seventy three,
So I hope you're partying in Heaven above,
With Dad and rest of the family!

*^♠♠♠^**^♠♠♠^**^♠♠♠^*

The Path of Righteousness!

To walk the Path of Righteousness, is what we're here to do!
Most find it very hard, but a few can just float through!

We're on the Path of Righteousness, as soon as we are born,
It is not a smooth road, there's pot holes to make you scorn!

There are obstacles and trials, all along the way,
That to carry on we all have to face, day by day!

It's not like every other path, to see where you're going,
Our path's are never same, so there is no map made showing!

The path is never-ending, while we live we struggle through,
Its rough, hard, mountains to climb, and cracks to swallow you!

But then as life is ending, when we think we're almost there,
That is when we see it change, to a lovely golden stair!

Stairs that take no climbing, for each step we hover over,
Till we reach the top and Heave to live, a life now in clover!

*^⚜⚜♠^**^⚜♠⚜♠^**^⚜♠⚜^*

شش🔸شد🏰شد🔸شش

War Is a Sin To Mankind

What is the reason that you fight,
Are you so sure that you're right?
Really exhausted every peaceful way,

*^♠🏰♠^*

Is it so hard to hear what others say.
Surely it's better to talk things through,

*^♠🏰♠^*

And do what you expect your children to do.

*^♠🏰♠^*

Shake hands and stop falling out,
If you can't agree then do not shout.
Never fight to let temper fly,

*^♠🏰♠^*

Try walking away don't make other's cry,
Or shake your fist in a threatening way,

*^♠🏰♠^*

Make an effort to save your friend and play,
And if you can't, then just, step right back,
Never impose yourself, on another's track.
Keep your composure and wear a smile,
Is what we tell children, when facing a trial.
Now us grown ups, should Practice What We Preach,
Demonstrating to children, Peace We Can Reach!

*^♠🏰♠^**^♠🏰♠^**^♠🏰♠^*

A Rainy Day Brought Sunshine

A Rainy day brought sunshine,
Though there was none in the sky,
For the clouds were black and heavy,
Holding more rain in supply!

But this rainy day brought sunshine,
To us on that dark day,
For if it hadn't been raining,
We'd have gone a different way!

But because the rain was heavy,
And the wind was blowing hard,
We went into the forest, hoping,
The trees would act as guard!

Twas' there that we met you,
As you gathered to celebrate,
Under covered tables,
With many dishes on a plate!

As we passed you smiled and said, 'Hola!'
Would you like to have a drink?
We smiled and came to join you,
Then glasses our we did clink!

You were celebrating a friend's birthday,
With music and guitar,
We stayed with you that afternoon,
Not wanting to wander far!

ش♣شد🏰شد♣ششد

We met because with it raining bad,
You couldn't walk as you normally would,
So instead you had a gathering,
A celebration that was good!

The following Saturday we met you,
But this time to mountain walk,
Stopping once in a while to have,
Victuals and a talk!

Now it's quite a number of years ago,
Since that very bad rainy day,
When we went to the woods instead of,
The beach where we normally play!

So Thank God! It had been raining,
Else we wouldn't have met that day,
And the wonderful sunshine of friendship,
Wouldn't be here in our hearts to stay!

*^♠🏰♠^**^♠🏰♠^**^♠🏰♠^*

ﺷﺷﺷ♣ﺷ⇧ﺷ♣ﺷ♣ﺷ

I Love I Need I Believe

Sometimes I need to feel love,
To see it flowing in a flood,
Sometimes I need it so much to show,
Sometimes I need only to know!

I always want to feel it there,
I always need to know you care,
I always want it demonstrated by,
Little things to make me high!

*^♠⇧♠^*

I believe that love makes you complete,
I believe love should be your every heart beat,
I believe that love comes more in giving,
I believe that giving means forgiving!

*^♠⇧♠^*

I believe truly forgiving, done and seen,
Then your love for God is ever green!
I believe that love must be free to go,
Round in a circle and like a river flow!

*^♠⇧♠^**^♠⇧♠^**^♠⇧♠^*

ش♣ش♣ش🏠ش♣شش

My Belief

My
Belief
In the Lord,
Is that with love,
And true forgiveness,
We'll lighten up our soul!
To raise us to His kingdom,
Where we can live forever in,
Heaven where loving peace is the goal!

This goal that we must always strive for,
Is true forgiveness in our hearts,
Love and compassion for all
To reach the open door!
Of Heaven that waits,
For all who love,
Believing,
In Him,
God!

*^♠🏠♠^**^♠🏠♠^**^♠🏠♠^*

All Our Pets In Heaven

All the pets I've ever had are now in Heaven above,
Together each and everyone linked through love!
I told Tony our Jock was now back playing with Jinni and Fran,
The two dogs he played with when on earth and ran!
With Fran would come, Fay my own lovely special friend!
With Fay, Fritz and Frisky the link goes on without end!
So our Jock will never be on his own up above,
He'll run round and play with all the Pets we love!
Because he knew Jinni and our Jinni is the link,
To take him to all the other pets as quick as a wink!
Tony thought awhile about this then sadly he did say,
"Well! What about our poor Farny' when she goes away!
She didn't know any of those pets we had before,
So she'll not see them, she'll be alone forever more!"

So I thought what'll happen when Farny goes then said!
"ALICIA who we love is the link I see it in my head!
For Alicia played with Jock all those years he was here,
She's old now but Farny loves her and she does her my dear!

So Alicia is the link to take Farny through to all our others,
Then they'll be together in Heaven like sisters and brothers!
So when we go to join them we'll have them all back,
We'll all walk together again down that Heavenly Track!"

*^^⚜^**^⚜^**^⚜^*

شـ♣شـ🏛شـ♣شـ♣ششـ

For The Good Life To Go On

Trees that grow tall and proud,
Cast a shadow on the ground,
To protect young saplings below,
From the sun rays so they don't grow,
At too fast a pace like gallop,
Rushed so they never develop!

*^♠🏛♠^*

Saplings with no shade grow too fast,
But not in a way meant to last,
For then they're stringy, weak below,
So that's not how a tree should grow,
Growing time is needed by a tree,
To develop 'naturally!

*^♠🏛♠^*

Strong roots are needed to give strength,
Till it reaches out at full length!
Until fully grown it must fight,
For the sun to embrace its light!
Then when full grown it will give shade,
To younger saplings needing aid!

*^♠🏛♠^*

شد♣شد♠شد⛩شد♠شد♣شد

Like trees we people ought to be,
Standing upright for all to see!
Giving strong roots, protecting young,
To keep them in close and among,
Family that will help them grow,
At a pace not fast or too slow!

*^♠⛩♠^*

Trees allow young just enough light,
For them to grow while kept in sight!
We should do same not let kids be,
Running around loose wild and free!
At a young age when vulnerable,
Future then is unpredictable!

*^♠⛩♠^*

Trees are symbol of family life!
You can see why so, without strife!
For when sun shines they let light through,
When wind blows hard they protect too!
They show what to do in times bad,
With leaves lost they still stand glad!

*^♠⛩♠^*

Never crumbling, looking for the light,
That's above always in their sight!
Then sunshine out and young ready,
They watch them stretch tall and steady!
Having learned from parents they then,
Begin the process once again!

For The Good Life To Go On......
*^♠⛩♠^**^♠⛩♠^**^♠⛩♠^*

Hope, Peace & Contentment

You need Hope in your mind and Contentment in soul,
Total Peace in your heart, for God to find you whole!
Hope number one is easy, for you to go and find,
But then you must keep it, solidly in your mind!

*^♠🏰♠^*

Never let it get lost, or else you will be blue,
For without Hope in mind, then all is lost to you!
With Hope Peace is found, in the heart at number two,
But it's the hardest thing, to keep and make come true!

*^♠🏰♠^*

Because to find true peace, you must surely be rid,
Of hate and prejudice, without forgiveness hid!
Once you've conquered, Hope and found Peace at heart,
You will find number three, has now the boost to start!

*^♠🏰♠^*

For Contentment to be seen in you to lovingly flow,
Through your Soul so whole, with love making it glow!
Please keep these three things clearly in mind and heart,
Then Heaven will be there for you to find when you depart!

*^♠🏰♠^**^♠🏰♠^**^♠🏰♠^*

The Joy Of Farny'

```
          \/
        o o '
           '
      o ' o o '
           '
     o ' ' o " o
        o ' '
      o ' o ' '
      o ' ' o o o
```

If there's one thing I'd like to say,
It's thank you! God for Farny
C heers! Hip,Hip Hooray!
For bringing me joy
Happiness and a
Reason to go
Out to
Play!
(*
*)
(*
*)
(*
*)
(*
*)
(*
A lovely start to the New Year,
Two thousand and seven! Yippee!
(*(0)*)(*(0)*)(*(0)*)(*(0)*)*(0)*)(*(0)*)

61

Hi! I'm Farny

Who was it said I look like a rat, or a bat with, a body!
Well! You might look like me if your life had been so shoddy!
Wanted I was when tiny pup, held in the palm of one hand!
Till my second teeth came, then I didn't look, so grand!

For on my bottom set one tooth grew big and protruded too!
Lifting up my top lip, to give a permanent grin, at you!
My ears they just grew like bat's wings big for my head!
My eyes too are rounded and also too big I've, heard said!

Now when I was a year old I was abandoned on the road,
Lost, lonely and frightened with a heavy load,
Of puppies in my belly, for yes I was carrying young,
But I was just in time before life out of me was rung!

*^♠☖♠^*

Taken to a stray dogs home, a refuge that gave good care!
Saving my life they then put a chip underneath my hair!
People came to the refuge to choose a dog for their own!
But no-one ever looked at me, so I felt unloved and alone!

*^♠☖♠^*

62

ش‌ش♣ش‌ش🏛ش♣شش

Then after a night of fireworks exploding, giving me fright!
The next morning my heart, was beating with all it's might!
For a couple at the dogs home, looking at dogs suddenly,
Came over to my cage, smiling down at funny me!

*^♠🏛♠^*

Well! I know now that the date was January 1st 2007
This couple's old dog had died, so I too was now in Heaven!
Now that was only yesterday, but already I feel much love!
They've re-named me Farny! Saying I've fitted in like a glove!

*^♠🏛♠^*

Funny enough they love me, for my silly looking smile!
So now this once abandoned dog is having a life worthwhile!
The world is now my Oyster, I'm off to Spain, France, then UK Now
that's not bad going, is it? For me a Tenerife Stray!

*^♠🏛♠^**^♠🏛♠^**^♠🏛♠^*

COMMENT

After losing our old Westie dog Jock, Tony and I felt so empty, New years day
morning walking past the dogs refuge we called in and brought the one above
home for a two day trial, she's been as good as gold, trusting and clean...and
yes although she is no where near as pretty as a Westie to look at she as
already given us some joy... and in a way it's a comfort to know that Jocks
passing as allowed an abandoned dog to find a good home!
Tony called her Farny' after me as Farnsworth is my maiden name and Farny'
often my nick name!

I Bred My Own

When I was young I always wanted to be a lad,
For being a girl alone didn't make me glad!

I didn't like being singled out with a dress made to wear,
I hated having to stand while my Mam braided my hair!

No I didn't enjoy being the only girl at all,
When I went to other girls homes, to pay a call!

I know now I was envious of the sister's they had,
Seeing their bonding closeness always made me feel sad!

So I stayed away from girls as much as I could,
Thinking playing with my brothers and lads more good!

But then when my eldest brother got a sweetheart,
Her being a sister to me was like a new start!

Having her paint my nails and make up my face,
Made me love to see her come visit our place!

But sadly they broke up and she was gone,
Leaving me thinking that's another fickle one!

Now this was to happen again and again,
Leaving me thinking girls only brought you pain!

Then I got married and I had two little girls,
Sisters for each other and for me two pearls!

I watched them having all I wished I'd had,
Seeing them playing, sharing, hugging made me glad!

Now they are both married and we all live apart,
But my lovely daughters are always deep in my heart!

Now they're more than a daughter these days I see,
They're my friends and they're also a Sister to me!

So those years being young missing a sister, alone!
Doesn't matter now for I've got two, I bred my own!

*^♠️♠^**^♠️♠^**^♠️♠^*

ش♣ش♣ش♖ش♣ش♣ششد

My Princess's Day

We celebrated the Birthday, of the late Princess yesterday!
Now it's my turn to celebrate, one of my Princess's today!

For this is the anniversary of her birthday,
With a girl in the family all shouted hurray!

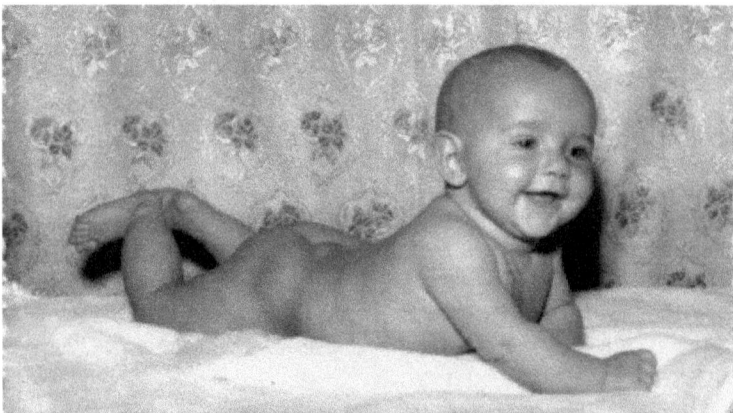

ش‌شد‌شد🏛ش‌ششد

Well! She brought us much joy, happiness and laughter,
And it wasn't long before she had us, her chasing after!

For she was running about, under a year old,
Which was pretty fast, at the time I was told!

Well she grew, learned and loved to ride a horse!
But the ones at the fair, not a real one of course!

As she'd rode she'd laugh, with joy so merrily!
But when they stopped she'd pout, for all to see!

شـ🍀شـ🍀شـⵜشـ🍀ششـ

But once on the beach, she would happily play,
Making sand pies and castles, with her Dad all day!

In fancy dress competitions she would have a go,
Dressing as Miss Turkish Delight! To steal the show!

Now as a woman, she is still much the same,
Full of enthusiastic energy, that helped make her name!

She's a Spiritual Healer, a Clairvoyant too,
With satisfied clients in countries world-wide I tell you!

68

ﺵﺷ♣ﺵﺷ🏰ﺵﺷ♣ﺵﺷ

Jeannette Du-Pont
She's taught me a lot, even though I'm her Mother,
With her as a friend, you don't need any other!

She's raising three darlings, Michael, Jack and Joe!
Alone to be as good and well behaved as any you know!

So on this, the Anniversary day, of our Jeannette's birth!
I have sent greetings to tell her, how I value her worth!

I love her! She knows it! So all that's left to say!
Is Jeannette you have a most wonderful day!

*^♠🏰♠^**^♠🏰♠^**^♠🏰♠^*

ش ♣ شد ♣ شد 🕌 شد ♣ شد ♣ شد

God Does Not Make Junk

You were born beautiful, with a soul of love,
That's come here to visit from the light above!
The reason you come is so you can learn,
That real true loving means you'll never spurn!

*^♠🕌♠^*

Any other living soul be it animal or man,
You must accept all to let your heart span!
Outwards and upwards so you embrace with love,
Everything on Earth and in the sky above!

You're a child of God, remember this always,
He doesn't make junk but he always says!
You have free will to follow if you please,
Up the road of love or the way of ease!

*^♠🕌♠^*

The easy route downhill where temptations call,
And where the Devil waiting for one and all!
Yes! Understand you will have slip and a slide,
For the crafty Devil will in disguise hide!

*^♠🕌♠^*

ش♣شد🏠شد♣شش

Temptingly and teasingly he will appear at every bend,
Till you're his, truly lost, then all the pleasures end!
With you left to wallow in his pit of despair,
While he's off to catch another one for his lair!

*^♠🏠♠^*

But always remember if you've been a fool,
That you've only been used as the Devils tool,
That while you breathe you still have a soul,
That can repent to love again and become whole!

I'll never forsake you anytime, just look for my light,
Forgive yourself and then let me hold you tight!

*^♠🏠♠^**^♠🏠♠^**^♠🏠♠^*

71

Double Celebration

Today's Deborah's birthday, so it's my anniversary too,
Of the day I love to celebrate, my Giving birth to you!

Forty five years ago, I had you my youngest child,
You've always been a sweetheart, never running wild!

You always knew how to cheer, make me laugh and smile,
Then you'd just shrug your shoulders, in a way to beguile!

ﺷﺪﺷﺪﺷﺪﺷﺸﺪ

Though you couldn't speak right for you had a stammer,
This you overcame, now people worldwide clamor!

To book you to speak, for you are known whole world wide,
In the art of astrology, where you stand to talk with pride!

You're always so accomplished, in everything you do,
So yes! I am so happy, on the anniversary of having you!

Deborah Houlding.

Hugs!

*^♠♙♠^**^♠♙♠^**^♠♙♠^*

ش‍شش‍شش‍شش

The Ship I Saw Sailing

The ship I saw sailing in the blue,
Was full of many people that I knew,
I saw my Mother, Father, brothers and then,
Grandparents and more from way back when!

*^♠⇧♠^*

The ship was on a journey to come for more,
I hoped it me as I stood on shore,
But then I saw a great big wisp of cloud,
Covering the ship to hide the crowd!

*^♠⇧♠^*

Whilst in the cloud the ship it turned course,
To sail away off in the blue with force,
I just stood and waved with tear in eye,
They all waved back for they heard my cry!

*^♠⇧♠^*

Then I heard my Granddad standing on deck.
Telling them all to keep themselves in check,
I saw Dad comfort Mam and guessed he said,
"It's not time for our Pat she must stay in bed"

*^♠⇧♠^*

Then as the ship sailed off in the blue,
They waved Granddad shouted "We love you!
We'll sail here again don't be afraid,
Next time we will see that your ticket's paid!

*^♠⇧♠^*

ﺷﺷ♣ﺷ🏰ﺷ♣ﺷﺷ

Till then wake up Pat and enjoy your life,
The illness is past that caused you strife,
Enjoy your life with the family you have there,
Show how life is best when love you share."

*^♠🏰♠^*

The ship then sailed o'er horizon blue,
They waved, my eyes opened, I came to,
To see grandchildren standing by me,
Smiling with joy so lovingly!

So happy am I now, that I glow,
For best of both worlds is mine I know,
With the love of children here on Earth,
Plus my Parents in that other land of worth!

*^♠🏰♠^**^♠🏰♠^**^♠🏰♠^*

Who Do I Run To

When I thought I was losing Tony! T
These thoughts came in my head,
Please God! Make Tony better,
Please! Let me go first instead!

For I thought if Tony went first,
Then when it was my turn to die,
Who would I run to first?
These thoughts then made me cry!

For if Tony went before me,
I'd have two husbands above,
Two father's of my children,
Two men that I love!

So if they were both there before me,
Which one would I first run too?
That's when I started to cry because,
I didn't know what I'd do!

ﺷﺷ♣ﺷ🏰ﺷ♣ﺷ

For I wouldn't want to hurt one,
By running first to the other,
When I love them both truly equally,
Like I do all those I call brother!

So who would I turn to first?
With these thoughts I lay crying in bed,
When all of a sudden,
I heard a voice and it said!

"If you get to Heaven, then you are full of love,
You are a soul not a body, that's how it is above!
You will embrace together, each other and all,
Love you'll find in Heaven has no dividing wall!
Only on Earth is there division, by sex, color and creed,
But here up in Heaven, these things they have no need!
For to rise above to this height, you will surely be,
Full of love totally for everything you see!
So don't worry, who goes first, for when you're above
You will be truly welcomed, by everyone with love."

Later when I told Tony these reasons why I wished I go first, He just
replied, it won't bother me if you embrace Harold first, He was your
first husband I would just wait till you'd done, then I'd embrace you...
so stop your silly worries!..
That's LOVE!

*^♠🏰♠^**^♠🏰♠^**^♠🏰♠^*

When Silence Isn't Golden

One step forward two steps back,
That's how I hate walking on the track,
Better be drunk then we might see,
A wobbling side to side by you and me!

*^♠🏰♠^*

For at times it don't rain but what it pours,
And all that's seen is slamming of doors,
A fighting done by walking away,
Only takes it through into another day!

*^♠🏰♠^*

Silence isn't golden when hard to take,
When purposely done to hurt and break,
This silence isn't static it simmers in a pot,
Till it boils over and like war hits a lot!

*^♠🏰♠^*

For this is not a quick battle said and done,
This is a making of war hurting everyone,
All who are close and in between,
Will be hurt by the pain that is seen!

*^♠🏰♠^*

So if you are hurting don't keep it hid,
Or walk away like you did as a kid,
Just let all out what is on your mind,
Then hopefully together answers you'll find!

*^♠🏰♠^*

Even if the worst happens and you shout,
Bellow, rant and rage at least it'll be out,
In the open, then once passion spent you'll see,
You can calmly, talk it over with a nice cup of tea!

*^♠🏰♠^**^♠🏰♠^**^♠🏰♠^*

78

شد♣شد🏰شد♣ششد

FAITH

Dear God I don't know where I'd be,
If there was no Faith in me!
For Faith is Hope,
Hope is Love,
Love is You up above!

Faith is something that we can't see,
Faith we know, is necessary!
Like the air,
We breathe each day,
It's not seen but we need it and pray!

That uncontaminated liberally,
It will always be flowing free,
Like your Love,
That we with Faith know,
Is always there, if in Faith we grow!

To feel your touch with no pressing might,
To see even though we have no sight,
To know with Faith,
What we feel is love,
To see the light that's You above!

This we do when we have

FAITH

*^♠🏰♠^**^♠🏰♠^**^♠🏰♠^*

79

ﺷﺪﻣﺷﺪﷺﺷﺪﻣﺷﺸﺪ

I Thank you

This is a poem that I put online,
That I wish to be simply divine,
To express all what is dear to me,
So I'm starting with my family.

For each and everyone I adore,
Be they close or on a far away shore.
They are all deep within my heart,
With love to stop me falling apart.

When things are bad, to them I cling,
In my darkest hour, light they bring.
I am Blessed I believe that's true,
And I know Dear GOD it comes from you!

For the love I have, within my heart,
I'm not meant to keep, but with it part,
By loving, caring, sharing and giving,
To everything and all that's living!

So this I try each day to do
By expressing love that's come through,
It's me saying in my own special way,
'Thank You' GOD for hearing me pray!

For being there always, watching above,
Over me and mine, and all the family I love!
With this I include all the family of man,
Out in the world, wherever they span!

And all the creatures on land, sky and sea,
The Earth, Sun, Moon and the Stars we see!
For everything comes from you my LORD,
To link us and giving us a common cord!

Everywhere I look, wonders I see,
All created by you which pleasures me!
Now there's nothing much more that I can add,
Except writing this poem as made me glad!

*^♠♕♠^**^♠♕♠^**^♠♕♠^*

ﺷﺪ♣ﺷﺪ🏠ﺷﺪ♣ﺷﺸﺪ

Dear God

Let your loving light shine down this night,
To ...... touch ...... Daveda's .... Family!
With healing strength clean and bright,
For her loved ones to gain,
Peaceful rest then see
Hurt ... diminished
All pain eased,
With LOVE!
GOD

LOVE
Builds...it's
Strength giving
It ... eases ... pain
So... we rise...above
Material .... hurting
To let Soul's be clearly seen
In...the aura of each...person
Shining bright, glowing ready for GOD
!
*^♠🏠♠^**^♠🏠♠^**^♠🏠♠^*

81

شد♣شد⇑شد♣شش

Take Jesus for A Ride

On the day after Christmas
At a church in San Francisco,
Baby Jesus went missing,
And no-one saw him go!

*^♠⇑♠^*

All the other figures were there,
The lambs and Joseph and Mary,
But no little baby Jesus,
To make the congregation wary!

*^♠⇑♠^*

The Priest he quickly ran outside,
And a little boy he soon did see,
Pushing his new red wagon,
As happy as could be!

*^♠⇑♠^**^♠⇑♠^**^♠⇑♠^*

Inside the wagon was Jesus,
The Churches figurine,
So the Priest walked up to the little boy,
Asking, Hello where have you been?!

Tell me my boy where did you get,
Your passenger for a ride?"
"I went into the church, Sir,
And I got him from inside!"

*^♠🏠♠^*

"Well why did you take him,
The Priest asked in shock"
"I took him to give him,
A little ride around the block!

*^♠🏠♠^*

Because a week before Christmas,
I went and prayed to Jesus there,
Saying if I get a wagon this Christmas,
I'll give you a ride to show I care!"

*^♠🏠♠^**^♠🏠♠^**^♠🏠♠^*

83

ﺷﺸﻪﺷﺸﻪﺷﺸﻪﺷﺸﻪﺷﺸ

A Tree and Christmas

There is something I love to see,
That GOD made and it's a tree,
Growing in clusters that we call a wood,
Especially in spring, when they start to bud.

*^♠⛪♠^*

And there is something I hate today,
That's how man is clearing them away.
Ridding the Earth of beautiful growth,
To create the unbalance, we all loathe.

*^♠⛪♠^*

So let's all now start and protect the tree,
And I hope that you'll do the same as me,
Because' I'm going to try now very hard,
To buy recycled paper and cut down on card,

*^♠⛪♠^*

Starting this Xmas cards I won't send,
To all on Internet family or friend,
I'll e-mail them a poem like this one to you,
With the message I want to come through.

*^♠⛪♠^*

That I hope this Christmas two thousand and six,
Brings Joy, Love, Happiness and all problems fix,
That the Joy experienced during these special days
Will overflow to the New Year and stay always.

*^♠⛪♠^**^♠⛪♠^**^♠⛪♠^*

'Mary Ann's Fears'

At nursery school little Mary Ann,
Was told Santa Claus comes if he can,
To all little children who have been good,
Flying through sky on his sleigh of wood.

Pulled by reindeers who stop beside,
The chimneys where children live inside.
Then when all in bed Santa does crawl,
Down the chimney with a toy for all.

All the kids excited just could not wait,
Each day ripping off the advent calendar date,
All except little Mary Ann who looked blue,
The teacher noticing said "Mary Ann do!

*^♠⥮♠^*

ﺷﺪﮊﺷﺪﮊﺷﺪﮊﺷﺪﮊﺷﺸﺪ

Please tell me child why you look so sad,
Santa's coming soon why aren't you glad?"
"You said he comes down the chimney Christmas night,
To give a toy to every good children in sight!

*^♠⬆♠^*

Well he's not coming to see me I know he's not,
Because I've looked and a chimney we haven't got,
So what is the point of me being good,
If he can't come to me on his sleigh of wood!"

*^♠⬆♠^*

But he will come to you; you're a very good girl,
There is no obstacle that Santa can't unfurl,
For those without a chimney living in a flat,
Santa can magically get around that!

*^♠⬆♠^*

He'll come through the window no matter how high,
While his reindeers wait above in the sky,
There is not one child will be missed that night,
For he loves everyone that is in his sight!

*^♠⬆♠^*

At this little Mary Ann's smile appeared,
Much re-assured now she no longer feared,
Being left out of the Christmas joy,
And she started to pray for a special toy!

*^♠⬆♠^*

Each day now eager to check the date,
Making the advent calendar task her fate,
Then on the morn of Christmas day,
She hugged the doll Santa had brought her way!

*^♠⬆♠^**^♠⬆♠^**^♠⬆♠^*

Passion for Poetry

Poetry can bring out
All the help needed when hurting,
Secrets once released will heal, to
Show, your loving inner light burning.
It is the music that will
Open your Soul's door to,
Navigate the inspiration there within you.

*^♠⬗♠^*

Flowing with syllable count,
Or acrostic to let title fall,
Rhyming or free verse matters not at all.

*^♠⬗♠^*

Poems that are written
Open up emotions to,
Etch thoughts in the mind ,
To help other's that read you!
Releasing your true self to see,
Your Soul laid bare!

*^♠⬗♠^**^♠⬗♠^**^♠⬗♠^*

شد♣شد🏰شد♣ششد

A Child Prays

A
Candle,
Sends out its
Rays, just like a
Kneeling child that prays!
Asking Our Father to,
Bless us all and send us peace,
So that we see all wars now cease!
God Bless the Children, who pray this way,
For they've seen through the light of day,
They've been taught about the love,
That we get from above!
Children that pray are,
Heard by Angels,
From afar,
Such is
Love!

*^♠🏰♠^**^♠🏰♠^**^♠🏰♠^*

Looking for Trouble

Never trouble, trouble,

Till trouble troubles you,

Or you will find that trouble,

Is always troubling you!

*^♠⬕♠^*

When troubles not about,

Then let trouble be gone,

Forget that she's ever been,

And start having some fun!

Patricia's Harmony

PEACE WILL COME FOR ALL,
AND LIFE EVERLASTING TOO,
THROUGH LOVE TRULY SHOWN!

*^♠⛪♠^*

RIGHT WILL COME TO STAY
IF WE ALL JUST LIVE WITH FAITH,
CHOOSING THE LORD'S WAY!

*^♠⛪♠^*

INSPIRING HIS LOVE
ACCEPTING THAT HE LOVES ALL,
SHOWING WE DO SAME.

*^♠⛪♠^*

HELPING OTHERS SEE,
ALL THAT WRONGED THEY CAN STILL BE,
RAISED AND FORGIVEN!

*^♠⛪♠^*

MAKING THE DECISION TO WALK,
ON THE PATH OF LIGHT THAT IS LOVE
NEVER FORGETTING THOSE IN NEED
YOU WILL THEN SEE HEAVEN ABOVE!

*^♠⛪♠^**^♠⛪♠^**^♠⛪♠^*

This is a style of poetry invented by the poet
Christina R Jussaume
As a friend to honor my name it is formed using 4 senryu's followed by
a four line verse 8syllables on each line in acrostic form of the title:
Patricia's Harmony...must be spiritual in content...

ﺷـﺷـﺷـﺷـﺷـﺷـﺷـ

Think Of Me

When you're down in the depths feeling low,
Thinking you've no place to go,
Think of Me! To grow!

When you have a pain in the gut,
Cause' your life's in such a rut,
Think of Me! Trust Put!

When you think you're heart won't mend,
And you're desperately in need of a friend,
Think of Me! To depend!

For I will ever and always be here for you,
To help you heal and see it through,
Think of Me! Please do!

For if you do then I know, you'll find,
More contentment in your mind,
Think of Me! Be kind!

For I'll willingly share all the hurt and pain,
That brings your tears to fall like rain,
Think of Me! You'll gain!

Because when you have with me shared,
All the things that's made you scared,
I'll pray to God that healings sent,
To make you happy and content.
So never think you are on your own,
With troubles escalated and overgrown,
For I am here and will always be,
Willing to help as you will see,
Think of Me! Eternally!

*^♠🎁♠^**^♠🎁♠^**^♠🎁♠^*

ششششﭐشش

My Floral Rainbow

White: Daisies I've loved ever since a child,
Red: Poppies that grow in the meadow wild!

Orange: Tiger lilies so vividly strong and bright,
Yellow: Daffodils with trumpets that give delight!

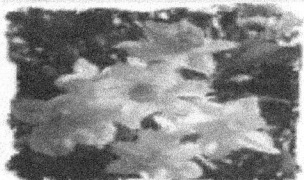

Green: Grasses plain and ornamental to show,
Blue: Bluebells carpeting woods with a cheery hello!

Indigo: Lilac to remind of Grandmothers care,
Violet: Forget-me-not's that grow here and there!

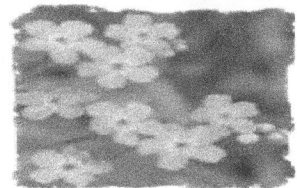

This is the floral rainbow I love to see,
That the Gardener planted to please you and me!

Seeing what the Gardener's done make me say,
"Thank you God for this floral array"

*^♠⇧♠^**^♠⇧♠^**^♠⇧♠^*

93

Heaven's Gold

There is lots of gold in Heaven, but mining is never done!
For it has no monetary value and it's shared by everyone!

The gold that's seen in Heaven isn't in nuggets but light!
Shining in the auras, of loving Souls so bright!

In Heaven there are no storms to create violent eruption,
Everything runs smoothly, for there is no corruption!

There is no need of radar or batteries to generate,
Or electricity to give light or power to operate!

In Heaven each Soul as a built in TV screen and computer,
With pictures and thoughts sent out through its special router!

In Heaven air is crystal clean, with no pollution to cause decay,
No gassy fumes to making black clouds to color the sky grey!

Everything that's growing there is fed by God's own hand,
He irrigates the pasture so all you see is fertile land!

So everything in Heaven is always a healthy green!
Showing the best of natural beauty that ever can be seen!

94

With flowers in abundance making the most colorful array,
With trees that blossom continually to match them in display!

In Heaven religion doesn't segregate, nor politics divide,
No ruling inflated personas seen, strutting about with pride!

For in Heaven there's only LOVE, Energy so light,
Made stronger by Souls up there helping to keep it bright!

All honoring the one GOD the creator of all,
The GIVER of loving worth free for all who call!

Now calling on HIM is easy all you ever need do,
Is say, "God please forgive me and show the way through"

Then just take a step at a time getting through each day,
Keeping Him always in sight till you find the way!

For Our God is all forgiving! All He asks of you is LOVE,
That's the only key ever needed to get in Heaven above!

But it has to be made of pure LOVE, shown to ALL by you!
Giving forgiveness where needed, just like GOD portrayed true!

A Heart
Forgiving

*^♠🏠♠^**^♠🏠♠^**^♠🏠♠^*

شد♣شد🏰شد♣شد♣شد

Special Friends

A very special relationship,
You can see comfortably sit,
Just as it always has,
With a Canadian and a Brit,
Then for a perfect triangle,
There's the Americans too,
All joined together with love,
Helping each other through!

This great friendship forged,
Over many, many years,
Built on happy celebrations,
Struggles, hardship and tears!
But the bond this created,
Is like a family strong,
Each an individual,
Yet Happy' to belong!

*^♠🏰♠^*

ش♣ش♣ش🏠ش♣ش♣شش

Now a very special friendship,
Is again seen to be,
Created through poetry,
By Daveda and me!
When we met in Toronto,
We immediately formed a bond,
Now this as grown and grown,
To feelings more fond!
A Canadian and a Brit,
American Sonny there too,
With Tony making our triangle
Into a square true!

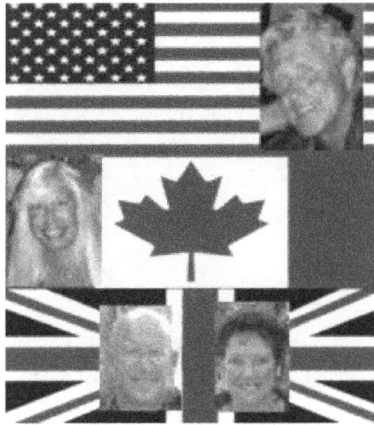

Yes! I believe it's wonderful,
When loving friendships grow,
Between folk who are faraway,
Yet close enough to let love flow!

*^♠🏰♠^**^♠🏰♠^**^♠🏰♠^*

ﺷﺸ♣ﺷﺪﺷﺪﺷ♣ﺷﺸﺪ

When two Hearts Beat as One

When people know what love is,
Their hearts become one!
This as always been the way,
Ever since time begun.

*^♠️♠^*

That is what true love is,
Two hearts beating as one,
Always and ever,
Not now and again for fun!

And it isn't just lovers,
That has this special gift,
It's same with brothers, sisters, friends,
Even if they are adrift!

~*^♠️♠^*

In faraway countries,
Over sea in far off land,
Two hearts can still pulsate with love,
As if walking hand in hand!

*^♠️♠^*

Hearts can always beat as one,
Wherever like is found,
Likeness in true loving,
In wanting to give it ground!

*^♠️♠^*

ﺷﺸﺷ🏛ﺷﺷﺷ

For it's not the mind that binds all,
So stop letting it rule,
Your actions toward others,
By thinking it is cool!

*^♠🏛♠^*

If you've loving in your heart at all,
Even if only for yourself,
Then concentrate on that love,
To see it escalate with wealth.

*^♠🏛♠^*

The wealth of knowing what love is,
And then when this as been found,
You'll find you love more than yourself,
But others all around!

*^♠🏛♠^*

Then seeing other's in despair,
Will touch your own heart too,
To let the love inside it,
With care come pouring through!

*^♠🏛♠^*

Love can bind each and everyone,
So let it purely flow,
Then we'll see warring situations,
Just dissolve and go.

Love it makes the world go round.

*^♠🏛♠^**^♠🏛♠^**^♠🏛♠^*

The Church On The Hill

High up on a hill
A church has been built with love!
What an achievement!

*^♠⛪♠^*

Achievement that shows,
Shows all that look up,
Up towards the light
Light is where there's love,
Love needs to be shown,
Shown by endeavors,
Endeavors that build,
Build so we can grow,
Grow nearer to God,
God then high above,
Above looking down,
Down to see the church!

*^♠⛪♠^*

This sheer effort achieved on the hill,
Was done by man struggling with great will,
No machinery taking,
The load off backs breaking,
Accomplishing the dream to fulfill!

*^♠🏛♠^**^♠🏛♠^**^♠🏛♠^*

Man did the work

Like an Angel

The Church in picture is in the South of France!

An Haiku 5 7 5 syllables with last word starting
a 12 line chain poem
(Chain poem as last word starting the next line)

Finishing with a limerick on the subject 9 9 6 6 9 syllables.

*^♠🏛♠^**^♠🏛♠^**^♠🏛♠^*

101

The Moon Above

The moon had a wonderful BLUE glow,
That shone SILVER down on the sea,
Making BLACK volcanic sands,
Awash... with ...mystery!
As... the WHITE ...foam,
Laps on the shore,
I... just... feel
Such happy
Joy!

*^♠🏛♠^*

Joy
That fills,
Me with peace
So ...that.... I feel
I... am.. in ..the... PINK,
Then as the dawn comes in,
With... RED shining...in the... sky,
The GOLDEN sun... appears so bright,
To once again fill me....... with delight!

*^♠🏛♠^**^♠🏛♠^**^♠🏛♠^*

Nature's Cycle in Nonets

The GOLDEN sun brings us new spring warmth,
To turn the trees ………a lovely GREEN,
Then blossom comes cherry PINK,
For fruit in ….summer seen!
Apples……… rosy RED,
Grapes juicy BLACK,
Till… autumn
Shows all
Gone!

*^♠🏠♠^*

Then
…Winter…
Comes trees bare,
Jack Frost … is near,
WHITE snow falls on ground,
Then everything's ………. frozen,
Till spring's warmer……sun is found!
To shine in…..BLUE skies …… up above,
That's nature's cycle …… each season …Loved

*^♠🏠♠^**^♠🏠♠^**^♠🏠♠^*

شد♣شد♣شد🏛شد♣شد♣شد

Figment of My Imagination

There once was a beautiful maiden that caught the Duke's eye,
So he sent his men to get her, even though he heard her cry!
It was true she was outstanding, among all the other maids,
With bright blue azure eyes and golden hair that did cascade!

*^♠🏛♠^*

Though kept her captured, he couldn't make her loving think,
Just like the horse you take to water, you cannot make drink!
The more that she spurned him the nastier he would be,
Slapping her until weakly she wept, then taking her forcibly!

*^♠🏛♠^*

She hated the big fat ugly Duke, who stank like sour wine,
And gradually as weeks went by, for death she began to pine!
One Sunday in the Cathedral while he took the wine and bread,
The Maiden took chance to flee, walking up the Tower instead!

*^♠🏛♠^*

The Duke's men seeing her thought nothing much of it at all,
Till the Duke returning to his pew, her name began to call!
The men gave chase immediately, but fast the Maiden ran,
To the very top window, with jumping out being her plan!

*^♠🏛♠^*

شد♣شد♣شد🏛شد♣ششد

This she did just as the men, came running too late to grab,
Flying through the air to land at the Duke's feet like a crab!
Just before she hit the ground, he saw her most beautiful face,
Smilingly lit by a wonderful light, at seeing Heaven's grace!

*^♠🏛♠^*

When her body hit the ground, He looked at the sky not down,
He knew where she'd gone from him, this made him frown!
For he knew he'd never see her again, for he would never go, To that
place where she'd gone because of his actions so,

*^♠🏛♠^*

He recalled when he saw the bright light that he also heard,
Wonderful voices singing out loud, the Hallelujah word,
Yet no one was in the Cathedral all were out taking a look
So he knew the voices were Angels much spoke of in the book!

I was challenge by another poet to choose a picture
then write an inspired story/poem about it.
My picture is of the cathedral in the town of Uzes France
where I love to spend summer...

*^♠🏛♠^**^♠🏛♠^**^♠🏛♠^*

Love for Angelwowings

This is a prayer poem to show much love,
To Angelwowings who has lost to above,
Her Father for whom we all did pray,
He got his healing he's in Heaven today!

One hundred percent worth to make him light,
For the Angels to take him home in flight,
Up to more loved ones who have waited above,
A long time to welcome this man they love!

So Angelwowings Dad is now okay,
But she is left feeling the loss today,
So friends I now ask that you join me,
In prayers for Our Sister for strength see!

Pray that she'll feel the comforting arms,
That will help her stand tall and show her charms,
Up to her Father who's now above looking down,
Cause' a smile will reward him much more than a frown!

So Angelwowings, my sweet friend, Dear,
Give your Dad a smile be it through a tear!
Let the loved ones that care for you up above see,
That you know they're around you constantly!

Yes! I wrote this poem specially my friend for you!
Because I have suffered this same loss too,
So I understand and I want you to know,
That I'm here for you if you need a friend so!

*^♠♟♠^**^♠♟♠^**^♠♟♠^*

I wrote this for a poet friend who writes under the pseudonym
Angelwowings hoping to give comfort on the day her daddy died.

شد♣شد♣شد⚜شد♣شد♣ششد

What is Faith

Faith is hope, faith is love,
Faith is strength from Him above!
Faith comes with true believing,
Forgiveness you will be receiving!

*^♠⚜♠^*

Faith can build, faith can grow,
Faith can spread if you let it show!
Faith can create, faith can guide,
Forever so you walk with pride!

*^♠⚜♠^*

Faith can lift, faith can move,
Faith can lift you out the groove!
Faith is man with inner wealth!
For faith in God brings faith in self!

*^♠⚜♠^**^♠⚜♠^**^♠⚜♠^*

ش‍‍ش‍‍ش‍‍🏰ش‍‍ش‍‍ش‍

Now And Then

As I lay in my garden on the grass so green,
I think of my life and all that I've seen,
As I look at the sky and the golden sun,
I think of folk here and those who are gone!

*^♠⬆♠^*

Since nineteen forty I have seen some change,
Things that's been good to rearrange,
I've watched things grow; I've seen things die,
Many things that make me wonder why?

*^♠⬆♠^*

Now as I reflect on the past I've had,
I think those times now not so bad!
When we had no car but walked instead,
Down country lanes with Hawthorn hedge!

*^♠⬆♠^*

With friends round the corner if we'd something to say,
We'd see them in person and pass the time of day!
With loved ones far away we'd write them words to keep,
To treasure even if, it made them laugh or weep!

*^♠⬆♠^*

شدهشدهشدهششد

Going to the pub was the traditional thing done,
With a piano in the corner we'd sing and have fun,
With many different folk doing their own party piece,
Tell me! Why did these happy times have to cease?

*^♠♤^*

Instead of country lanes now we have tarmac roads
Getting wider and wider to accept heavy loads!
Then the cars are parked jam packed in the street,
Where former kids played under lamp to meet!

*^♠♤^*

Now they sit on the settee for conversation,
All alone by text to every friend or relation!
Singing round a piano in the pub now is gone,
But at least Karaoke can create some fun!

*^♠♤^*

Yes! There are many things and times I recall,
But most happiest moments of them all,
Was seeing friends and neighbors greatly rejoice,
Singing all together with one voice!

*^♠♤^*

My Gran always said; "When they go out singing,
They come back home singing, with voice a ringing"
So let us encourage more singing today then I say,
To get old fashioned happiness back to stay!

*^♠♤^*

Karaoke singing irritates a lot I know
But it's good to see the young sing, hearts aglow!
Let's keep them singing to get their fighting to cease,
With music in their hearts they might find peace!

*^♠♤^**^♠♤^**^♠♤^*

Holidays Are Important

Children playing on the beach,
As waves gently lap the shore,
Mums and Dads in happy repose,
Who could ask for anything more!

*^♠⭐♠^*

All those wanting a perfect tan,
Lay akimbo on the beach,
To turn a normal pallid skin,
Into a lovely golden peach!

*^♠⭐♠^*

Teenagers using their surf boards,
To give other's a ride in the sea,
Still content to be on the water,
Even when there's no waves to see!

*^♠⭐♠^*

شد♣شد🏰شد♣ششد

But being in the sunshine,
With your family so carefree,
Is one of the greatest joys in life!
So enjoy it please like me!

*^♠🏰♠^*

For holidays are important,
It's the time of bonding together,
When you can let all worries go,
Not giving a fig or a feather!

*^♠🏰♠^*

But don't go spending a fortune,
Trying to live life like a king,
Remember a tent in the country,
Can just the same joy bring!

*^♠🏰♠^*

When you sit on a balmy evening,
Content after barbeque,
Watching the sun set in the sky,
With those you love all close to you!

*^♠🏰♠^**^♠🏰♠^**^♠🏰♠^*

ﺷﺷﺷﺷﺷﺷﺷﺷﺷ

A Cross To Bear

We all have a cross to bear at times in life,
Not letting it bury us that is our strife,
Though we'll fall and stumble, that is true,
Remember Jesus he did the same thing too!

*^♠⛪♠^*

Oh! Yes He stumbled and fell with all the weight,
But he picked himself up to face His fate,
With grim determination he carried on,
Praying the ordeal would soon be done!

*^♠⛪♠^*

Yes we really do have a cross to bear,
Sometime in life and we all take a share,
Some carry it young, some carry it old,
Many carry it more than once I'm told!

*^♠⛪♠^*

So when a turn is at your abode,
Just pick it up and help carry the load,
Try not to be envious when others are free,
Of the cross that you now have troubling thee!

*^♠⛪♠^*

ش♣شد♣شد🕌شد♣ششد

Many think the grass is greener over there,
Well! A lot of time it's true so we must share,
If we're in the place that's luscious and green,
Share to lift the burden off other's that's seen!

*^♠🕌♠^*

For most of the crosses carried in life,
Are all man made to give us strife,
So we must remove all that needless pain,
That's seen in the world again and again!

*^♠🕌♠^*

If we do we'll only then carry the load,
That is truly ours as we walk the road,
Through life on the pathway, truly meant,
Till THERE where halcyon days are spent!

*^♠🕌♠^**^♠🕌♠^**^♠🕌♠^*

113

شـ♣ـشـ♣ـشـ🏛ـشـ♣ـشـ♣ـشـ

A Special Breed

Poets are a special breed,
They come in every color,
In all shapes and sizes,
Thin breasted or fuller!

*^♠🏛♠^*

Yes! Poets are a special breed,
For when they write they move,
Putting feelings down on page,
To lift you out the groove!

*^♠🏛♠^*

With words they paint a picture,
To give hope and show they care,
They make you laugh but best of all,
Share words in loving prayer!

*^♠🏛♠^*

So if you are a Poet then,
Keep writing for others to read,
Because my friend it is true,
You are a Special Breed!

*^♠🏛♠^**^♠🏛♠^**^♠🏛♠^*

إشدﭽشدﱫشدﭽشد

Poets in Heaven

When we poets go to heaven, we'll have a real good time,
Hobnobbing with society that once on Earth did rhyme!

*^♠⇧♠^*

All the great Masters there, will be happy to share their gift,
Of their written poetry for they'll want us to get a lift!

*^♠⇧♠^*

But in Heaven words spoken, won't done by tongue,
But by the thinking powers of the group, you now belong!

*^♠⇧♠^*

When sat together in circle, each poet will be free to send,
A poetic thought straight out, with pictures that will blend!

*^♠⇧♠^*

For you to store in a book, within your Soul so deep,
Loving, sweet thoughts to treasure, open up and reap!

*^♠⇧♠^**^♠⇧♠^**^♠⇧♠^*

إشـ♣شـ♣شـ🏛شـ♣شـشـد

Growing Pain

The older we get more pain we bear, often suffering alone'
With pains so hard to bear, that are not really our own!
Our own pains are in our hips, back, neck and knee,
For rheumatics and arthritis, roam our joints so easily!

*^♠🏛♠^*

We have pains in our stomach, when it doesn't digest,
Then indigestion is the result, with pains in the chest!
But we suffer more than the pains, that come with being old,
With emotional pain we find to be, the hardest to behold!

*^♠🏛♠^*

Everyone has an emotional pain, this we see as we live life,
Loss of parents, loss of a friend, loss of husband or a wife!
The hardest pain to ever bear must be a child taken away!
Yet we know the Lord takes so we can meet again one day!

*^♠🏛♠^*

So life goes on and we suffer, then we suffer even more,
When seeing our kids suffering, each time they come indoor!
A tiny tot with scraped knee, we can make better with a kiss,
But when grown their pains can't be dealt with easy as this!

إشد♣شد♣🏛♣شد♣ششد

That is when we suffer most, when there's nothing we can do,
Except try to give comfort, as watch them struggle through!
For when they cry we cry, when they worry we do too,
With terrible heartache knowing, there is nothing we can do,

*^♠🏛♠^*

So then our pain is not for self, we're now feel the pain of two,
Then when grand kids come along, you worry for more it's true!
Yes often a hurting in the body, can be treated to make it go,
But emotional pain for kids never goes till a smile they show!

*^♠🏛♠^**^♠🏛♠^**^♠🏛♠^*

117

إشد♣شد♣شد🏰شد♣شد♣ششد

Hank & Christina!

Dear Father God in Heaven above,
Hear these words said to you with love,
In prayer for you to quickly send,
You're Healing Angels down to mend!

*^♠🏰♠^*

All the joints that gives Hank pain,
Let love lubricate them once again,
So that he can go forward with his life,
Free from worry, pain and strife!

*^♠🏰♠^*

Let his wife Christina see with joy,
He can move once more like a boy,
Carefree, pain free strong and able,
To clock more years on life's table!

*^♠🏰♠^*

Never asking for self but for others, she,
So full of faith prays constantly,
So Dear Lord let the prayers she's sent out,
Boomerang back with healing clout!

*^♠🏰♠^*

To give her a lift with the healing love,
She always prays for others to get from above!

*^♠🏰♠^**^♠🏰♠^**^♠🏰♠^*

118

إشدﺷﺪﺷﺪ🏠ﺷﺪﺷﺷﺪ

When Death Came To Visit.

Death came to visit like a friend,
To tell us our ways we must mend,
He said the time may not be right,
So I'm sorry if I've given you a fright!

But I come as a friend on this visit to you,
To tell you to watch the things you do!
You can't keep abusing your body so,
Or next time I come you will have to go!

*^♠🏛♠^*

So now you've seen me you take heed,
For if not then I'll be back with speed,
Next time it won't be to knock at your door,
I'll be taking you with me that's for sure!

*^♠🏛♠^*

So change your diet and mend your ways,
Then you'll live to see years not days,
For It's only twice I will call on you,
Once is to warn and the other's to do!

*^♠🏛♠^**^♠🏛♠^**^♠🏛♠^*

119

إشــشـ♣ـشـ🏛ـشـ♣ـششـ

It Starts At the Cradle

Good kids keep you young
Bad kids put years on you,
So young Mum's it's up to you,
To start as you mean to do!

*^♠🏛♠^*

For whatever you do with a baby,
If you spoil and don't check,
When your child is a three years old,
You'll be screaming "What the heck"

*^♠🏛♠^*

Then you'll have your work cut out,
Trying to undo all the wrong,
This can be done but its testing,
Even if you prove to be strong!

*^♠🏛♠^*

But usually it's the three year old
That wins cause' they're a step ahead,
They're the child you put on a pedestal
The one you so proudly bred!

*^♠🏛♠^*

That's when parents have truly lost it,
With kids dictating what they do,
What they want, what they won't have,
What time they go to bed too!

*^♠🏛♠^*

ﺷﺪﺷﺪﺷﺪﺷﺸﺪ

So with lost control of a three year old,
How will you ever control a teen,
For then it's too late for you to start,
Giving the discipline they've never seen!

*^♠♙♠^*

Now this is the time that you will say,
And if I hear you I'll agree,
That "This blooming child of mine
Is putting years on me"

*^♠♙♠^*

So the moral of this poem is;
Don't start when they're running around,
Start when in cradle a babe in arms,
For discipline to be found.

*^♠♙♠^*

Then when you have a three year old,
Four, five, six then you can,
At seven say you can see the making,
Of a very fine young man!

*^♠♙♠^*

I once heard my Dad say;
Now I know that it's true,
"You give me the boy till seven,
And I'll show the man to you!

*^♠♙♠^*

So if you don't want to have bad kids,
That will put years on you,
Mould them from the cradle,
Then they'll grow and be a pleasure too!

*^♠♙♠^**^♠♙♠^**^♠♙♠^*

إشد♣شد♣شد🏛شد♣ششد

What If

What If I hadn't been born a girl,
And I'd been another lad
I'd have gone down the pit,
A different life then I'd have had!

*^♠🏛♠^*

So now I'm glad I wasn't,
Born a lad at all,
Because my working life's been,
A far greater ball!

*^♠🏛♠^*

What if I'd gone down to London,
To audition for that show,
It might have gone okay,
But would have changed the life I know!

*^♠🏛♠^*

إشـشـشـشـشـشـشـشـشـشـ

And what if Harold Hadn't died,
When we were newly wed,
Would I have had my daughters,
With him instead!

*^♠⇑♠^*

And if so would my daughters,
Be the same as they are today,
Would they be, could they be?
Who can possibly say!

*^♠⇑♠^*

So why do we say What If,
And look back at all,
Tell me; would the horse have won the race,
If he hadn't took a fall!

*^♠⇑♠^*

You don't know and I don't know,
So what's the point in wondering?
And looking back for all you're doing,
Is giving today a plundering!

*^♠⇑♠^*

What's gone is done, what's done is past,
What's past is past and should stay there,
The life you had, the life you've lived,
Has been a life to share!

*^♠⇑♠^*

By changing just one thing,
Many repercussions would abound,
And the gaining of the one thing,
Would mean many losses found!

*^♠⇑♠^**^♠⇑♠^**^♠⇑♠^*

How Much Do I Love You

How MUCH do I love you,
Please don't ever ask,
Because for me to say
Is an impossible task!

When you can see
How much salt there is in the sea,
Or count the stars,
That twinkles over thee,
Then you will know
What you mean to me,
For the answer will be Double
All that you see!

My heart with love you will never see,
Overflow with love or tire of thee!

Even when I am gone from here,
My love for you will be constant Dear!

For the heart in my body is just a pump,
That when I rise above my Soul will dump!

For the love that was in my heart will be,
Now the loving source of light to carry me!

Away from you but to other's above
That feels for me like I do for you with love!

So how much do I love you yes! I can tell you true!
I'll love you all the way to Heaven, pass the skies of blue,
When there the distance will strengthen love more,
Which I promise I'll be sending to you by the score!

*^♠♛♠^**^♠♛♠^**^♠♛♠^*

إشــشد♣شد🕌شد♣ششد

Dear Father God

Dear Father God in Heaven above,
Please let your shining light of love,
Shine down from Heaven on to me,
Till my body's filled completely!

*^♠🕌♠^*

Then let it swiftly through me flow,
To help the love in my heart grow,
Then let this love be pumped around,
Just like blood in my body found!

*^♠🕌♠^*

With each breath I take let the air be,
Full of loving light to enter me,
Please let me receive this gift from above,
Till I inhale and exhale only love!

*^♠🕌♠^*

Then each breath I release please let it be,
Added to the light shining down from Thee!
So that my children and all I greet,
Take a share so they too, are complete!

*^♠🕌♠^*

In each word I speak let your love flow,
Into the ears of others to grow,
So that they too will be filled like me,
With pure shining love coming from Thee!

*^♠🕌♠^**^♠🕌♠^**^♠🕌♠^*

Dear God Let's See

Dear God on this New Year's Day,
Let us please see peace come our way!
Let a wave of love now flow right o'er,
Those that differ by the score!
So that we then see all men embrace,
Each as a brother of the Human race!

*^♠⏏♠^*

Dear God give the rich a sharing desire,
To help where there is poverty dire!
Let's see the dreaded diseases, killing man,
All wiped out by a new health giving plan!
Then let the vulnerable young and old,
Be embraced in the family's fold!

*^♠⏏♠^*

Let 2008 be the much needed start,
Of a loving growth within each heart,
And let that growth spread to replace,
The hate that's killing this earthly race!
All these things Dear Father that we ask,
We see being done as a love building task!

*^♠⏏♠^*

ش♣شـ🏛شـ♣ششـ

Let us see love of all man as a brother,
And the love of Earth as our Mother,
She's the one feeding us so let her be,
Replenished and growing Eternally!
To conclude Dear Father let your love reign great,
In the hearts of all through two thousand and eight!

*^♠🏛♠^*

Then let us see it grow forever more...Amen!

Happy New Year 2008.

*^♠🏛♠^*

Happy..... Healthy people!

New... Nourishing growth!

Year............ Young love!

For 2008 and I pray every other year to follow!

*^♠🏛♠^**^♠🏛♠^**^♠🏛♠^*

ﺷﺪ♣ﺷﺪ⬆ﺷﺪ♣ﺷﺪ

A Healing Prayer

Close your eyes and see the light,
That's there inside of you!
Be aware of your innermost self,
To feel calmness coming through!

*^♠⬆♠^*

Now as you breathe see this light,
Circle within you and grow!
Then when its in your blood stream,
Just gently let it flow!

*^♠⬆♠^*

Around your body as you relax,
Contentment you will gain,
With a glowing warmth felt inside,
Like a sweet refrain!

*^♠⬆♠^*

ششﮐشﮐشـ

This light that you are strengthening,
Is the light within your soul,
It's the link to Spirit and Guides,
Who come to help you with your goal!

*^♠⬠♠^*

Then when your completely relaxed,
Gently say a prayer,
Thanking the Lord and Spirit above,
For their everlasting care!

*^♠⬠♠^*

Then ask that help is sent to those,
With a great healing need,
Do this and ask whenever you can,
For prayer is a powerful deed!

*^♠⬠♠^*

Then when done say a soft, "Amen"
As you gently open your eyes,
The calmness and the love you feel,
Will make you realise!

*^♠⬠♠^*

That by opening your mind to Spirit,
You let them come in close,
To establish a wonderful link,
You'll never want to lose!

*^♠⬠♠^*

Just ten minutes that's all it takes,
For you to open up and give,
By giving you too will recieve,
Healing that will help you live!

*^♠⬠♠^**^♠⬠♠^**^♠⬠♠^*

Heaven and Hell on Earth!

I believe in Heaven and I believe in Hell,
I believe both we can find on Earth here as well!
For I know I found Heaven when I was just sixteen,
With my boyfriend in the hay so peaceful and serene!

When he told me he loved me and I gave my heart away,
Oh! Yes! It sure was Heaven that I had found that day!
That heavenly bliss stayed with me lingering on,
Till joy exploded once again with the birth of my son!

Oh! Yes! I was living in heaven right here on Earth,
A feeling so precious I couldn't express it's worth!
But my Heaven shattered one cold December day,
When God in His wisdom took my love away!

To leave me lost and drifting in a terrible abyss,
With Heaven just a memory for me to reminisce!
Not understanding truly about God and His ways,
I let sadness turn to bitterness to darken my days!

Then with clouded mind blackened without any light,
I couldn't feel sunshine or see the moon at night!
This was Hell on Earth for no joy could I see,
There seemed to be the Devil in the heart of me!

But thankfully my parents with their precious love,
Made me understand, there is a Heaven above!
Where we will be welcomed and where again we'll meet,
Loved one's gone before us who wait happily to greet!

Now though I know it can be Heaven here in this place,
Compared to the real thing it's just a taste we face!
To help us understand that Heaven's found with love,
That Hell's when we feel low staying till away we shove!

So in life we must keep loving, showing other's we care,
This way we'll taste Heaven until we finally reach there!

*^♠♚♠^**^♠♚♠^**^♠♚♠^*

شـ♣شد♣شد🏠شد♣شـ♣ششد

Years Fly

It only seems like yesterday, I was like this!

Why
Do the
Years at both,
Ends of life fly,
With every day
Passing so quickly by!
The minute's days, months and years,
Come and go fast like drying tears!

*^♠🏠♠^*

One day baby with need to be fed,
Then soon adult earning own bread!
Then years flow in steady pace
Till suddenly they race!
Like the early years,
When day, month year,
Rapidly,
Flow till,
Gone!

*^♠🏠♠^**^♠🏠♠^**^♠🏠♠^*

131

ﺷﺪ♣ﺷﺪ⛫ﺷﺪ♣ﺷﺪ

Rolling Hills and Meadows

Rolling hills, meadows, blue skies, gentle breeze,
Dancing in the grass, flirting with the trees!

*^♠⛫♠^*

Rivers gently rippling, where children like to play
Splashing to catch a fish, going home sunset of day!

Rabbits bobbing, hare chasing, birds singing lovely tune,
Happy with heat haze gone now serenading the moon!

*^♠⛫♠^*

Night time creatures play now, like lovers happy to spoon,
O'er rolling hills and meadows, shadows cast by silvery moon!

*^♠⛫♠^**^♠⛫♠^**^♠⛫♠^*

شـشـشـ🏰شـ♣شـشـ

God of Love

Dear GOD of love let your loving light,
Shine down on all the people tonight!

Let them absorb it through every pore,
So that it fills them down to the core!

Then leaders filled with your healing light,
May just want to talk instead of fight!

Then they may, eventually see,
Their opponent's reasons to agree!

Then with love they could work together,
With arguments light as a feather!

Concentrating only to preserve,
Peace forever knowing you they serve!

We pray that your loving light will stray,
Around the world every night and day!

To heal the sick in body and mind,
So a healthier outlook, all find!

You gave us life GOD to take a turn,
Having freewill the Devil to spurn!

So that when we choose to follow you,
We do so freely with wanting to!

So although you gave us much freewill,
I still pray that your loving light will!

Reach out to all those going astray,
So that they come to YOU any way!

*^♠🏰♠^**^♠🏰♠^**^♠🏰♠^*

Dear Father God Hear Us

Dear Father God hear us each day,
When silently to you we pray,
For those we love who are in need,
Please give them healing now with speed!

Let them this moment feel your touch,
To lift their soul, this will help much!
In giving them strength facing pain,
Making them want to fight again!

So easy it is to let go,
When the body is hurting so,
That is when you're most needed there,
To lift their souls and show you care!

Start the process by turning wheels,
To help them while their body heals,
Give the Doctors and carers too,
Healing wisdom in all they do!

So Father! When we pray by thought,
Let the vibrations sent be caught!
By the healing Angels above,
Who work in silence bringing love!

*^♠⇧♠^**^♠⇧♠^**^♠⇧♠^*

شد♣شد♣شد🏛شد♣شد♣ششد

Dear Lord! We Pray

Dear Lord! We pray you help us, hear the silent cry,
Of someone in distress, hiding the reason why!

Dear Lord! Help us when we see eyes drooping sad,
Realize they are the windows, showing hurt is bad!

Dear Lord! Help us understand, to feel other's pain,
So we know what to say, to help them heal again!

Dear Lord! Help us hear that silent cry screaming out,
Especially in young children raw to what life's about!

Dear lord! We can do this, with those we love at home,
But how wonderful to do it with the lost that roam!

Be they wandering the streets, looking desolate lost,
How great if we hearing cries, then took on the cost

Of being the one to help them, be it just a kind word,
One to give inspiration, to let them know we cared!

That their silent cry we heard, their unshed tears saw,
Their pain felt we share, so they're not alone any more!

Dear Lord! Help us to be, more intuitive, in every way,
So we can help those in need, who silently cry each day!

*^♠🏛♠^**^♠🏛♠^**^♠🏛♠^*

When I Was Young

When I was young, ten years felt like fifty,
But when I look back now I'm not so nifty,
(Fifty years seems like ten)

*^♠♤♠^*

When I was young, I needed my Mam and Dad,
Who were always there to make me glad!
(I was so blessed)

*^♠♤♠^*

Then I had children and they needed me,
Giving me great joy every day to see!
(So Wonderful)

*^♠♤♠^*

Now that they are older standing alone,
By raising a family of their own!
(I'm doubly blessed)

*^♠♤♠^*

Yes! I'm so happy they've grown for me to see,
Them standing independent not in need of me!
(Hold their heads high)

*^♠♤♠^*

For I brought them up to show much love,
For brother and sister and God above!
(With caring hearts)

*^♠♤♠^*

For I had my children that I love so,
Not to be in need of them but to let go!
(Fly the nest)

*^♠♤♠^*

*^♠👑♠^*

So now I am older I don't want to see,
Them wasting their years looking after me!
(Independency)

*^♠👑♠^*

Though I know they would if there's a need,
I hope when the time comes I go with speed!
(To Heaven that is)

*^♠👑♠^*

But it's good to be needed so while I am here,
I have my little dog 'Farny' to give me cheer!
(Unconditional love!)

*^♠👑♠^*

She needs me, loves me, she keeps me on the go,
And when I am tired she lies beside me also!
(Better than hot water bottle)

*^♠👑♠^*

Yes! It's truly great to be needed but not so good to need,
Just like it's better to give than it is to receive!
(All, except God's Love of course!)

*^♠👑♠^**^♠👑♠^**^♠👑♠^*

شد♣شد♠شد🏛شد♣شد♣شد

The Green Peace Call

Dear Father God I beg you hear,
This most important prayer of all,
That men on Earth will rally together,
To back the Green Peace call!

*^♠🏛♠^*

Please help us save our Planet,
From the danger that's predicted,
Help us find a way to live,
With consumption more restricted!

*^♠🏛♠^*

Please help us preserve the icebergs,
By healing the ozone layer,
Help us stop temperatures rising
By showing man does care!

*^♠🏛♠^*

Help us find the way dear God,
To live without being destructive,
Help us right the wrong we've done,
For the future to be constructive!

*^♠🏛♠^*

We know we're on a slippery slide,
Help us take grip before too late,
So calendars double the years seen,
For the future to celebrate!

Comment.
I wrote this many years ago but now with Japan whaling again
I think it most appropriate again today.

*^♠🏛♠^**^♠🏛♠^**^♠🏛♠^*

ﺷـﺷـﺷـ♣ﺷﺷﺷ♣ﺷﺷ

Laws of Heaven

There are no laws in Heaven, for there, is no need,
Of any protection from theft abuse or greed!
There is no land register for anyone to own,
Or a marriage license to make a partner shown!

*^♠♟♠^*

Laws are never needed in Heaven up above,
For no-one is ever there, unless they're full of love!
Love of all souls equally caring for all the same,
With no division or segregation anyone can name!

*^♠♟♠^*

There is no land or territory where all cannot walk,
There is no language spoken that all cannot talk,
There's no-one to judge us as we're there by invite,
By the Lord God, Our Father who does so with delight!

*^♠♟♠^*

To have us sit beside him or if we to, want walk free,
No laws are needed because Heaven is true liberty
Where only loving days spent in sunshine awaits
For you and me behind pearly Gates!

This picture is on the cover of my book
Nine Clouds To Heaven

*^♠♟♠^**^♠♟♠^**^♠♟♠^*

139

My Son Robert

I have a one and only son,
Robert is His name,
Named after my own Dad,
Who was happy I called him same!

Now this year 2008 in April
On the twenty-first,
We will have a celebration,
That to me will be a first!

For my first Baby he will be,
Fifty years of age,
For me it's another chapter in life,
Reached by turning a page!

For 50 years we've shared life,
Both happy times and sad,
Robert now I want you to know,
The man I see I'm proud of and glad!

*^♠⏏♠^*

As a Father of four a Granddad too,
It's time for you to celebrate,
You've worked hard through all the years,
So now make relaxing your fate!

You've always done what's been needed,
Now Son I say it's your time,
Let life begin once again,
To enjoy sunshine now not grime!

The best years of your life
We all know is when you're a kid,
The second best is now my lad,
When you're reaping from all you did!

With the struggle of raising a family,
Now behind you with them grown,
This is the time for you to say,
Now my life's my own!

Yes! Enjoy this new era in life
That starts on your birthday anew
Make the most of it in all you do.
To last the rest of your birthdays through!

Happy 50th Birthday Robert

*^♠🏛♠^**^♠🏛♠^**^♠🏛♠^*

شـ♣شـ↟شـ♣ششـ

Let Hearts Love All

Dear Father God let your loving light shine,
On all that has a heart like mine,
A heart that's full of love for you,
A heart that loves all others too!

*^♠↟♠^*

For folk who love God just like me,
Will love all others that they see,
So strengthen this love Lord and let it be,
Spread round the world generously!

*^♠↟♠^*

For I know that folk with a heart like mine,
Only pray for peace and your love divine,
Only want to see people living free,
Together in peace and harmony!

*^♠↟♠^*

Dear Lord there would never be wars seen,
If everyone would lovingly lean,
Towards accepting you are the same,
Whatever we call you whatever the name!

*^♠↟♠^*

ﺷﺷﺷﺷﺷﺷﺷ

Dear God let your loving light shine too,
Down on to those who don't know about you!
Let it search them out and fill their mind,
With thoughts to encourage them to find.

*^♠⬆♠^*

Love and acceptance for all we call man,
Every color, nationality that o'er the world span!
Dear God let all have a love we can see,
Because I love all, even if they hate me!

*^♠⬆♠^*

So please God let all who love like me,
Shine in your light for all to see,
How much better, life is for loving You!
That to truly do so, means loving others too!

*^♠⬆♠^**^♠⬆♠^**^♠⬆♠^*

Bottled Troubles

When you're upset feeling blue,
Seeing depression coming through,
Then the worst thing you can do
Is bottle it up inside of you.

*^♠⇧♠^*

Don't be like any champagne bottle,
Keeping feelings tight so they throttle,
For the day will come when they will pop,
Flow right out and never stop.

*^♠⇧♠^*

Emotions are like soda pop full of gas,
Once shaken up you will never pass,
Them off as happy if they're sad,
Or pretend they're good if they are bad.

*^♠⇧♠^*

Hiding troubles with a smile,
You might see work for a little while,
But there will always come the day,
When a smile isn't able to wash them away!

*^♠⇧♠^*

ﺷـﺷـﺷـﺷـﺷـﺷـﺷـﺷـﺷـﺷـﺷـ

So it is always best to let them flow,
Share them with the folk you know,
If the voicing of them you find hard,
Then put them in words just like a bard!

*^♠♙♠^*

Yes! If you write them down in poem or essay,
You are now handling them in a good way,
If feelings put in words flow in a flood
Then this way bad might do some good,

*^♠♙♠^*

For someone somewhere just might see,
The words you wrote so emotionally!
To help understand if they suffered like you,
That in spite of it all you can still pull through!

Writing them Down

Helps Get Rid

Troubles!

*^♠♙♠^**^♠♙♠^**^♠♙♠^*

ش‍ده‍شد‍شده‍ششد

'My Easter Thoughts

When Jesus died on the cross,
His Soul it rose above,
So the only thing they entombed,
Was a body with no Soul to love!

*^♠⬆♠^*

Then when Jesus met Our Father,
He held him in his arms so tight,
So that His Son immediately,
Absorbed his loving might!

Then He had a real good time,
Rejoicing with God and seeing,
All the lovely life up there,
Continuing, loving and being!

*^♠⬆♠^*

شد🌸شد🌸شد🏠شد🌸ششد

On the second night God said,
"Son! Tomorrow I want you to go,
Back down to that tomb,
To get in that body again to show!

*^♠🏠♠^*

All those people who loved you,
Your enemies too, will see,
That they could not killed the love,
You have in your heart for Me!

*^♠🏠♠^*

Then tell all that gather around,
That if they love me true,
They must also never fear death,
For they'll rise above like you!"

*^♠🏠♠^*

ﺷﺪﺷﺪﺷﺪﺷﺪﺷﺸﺪ

So Jesus came back down,
With His might he tore apart,
The tomb where they had put Him,
Thinking him dead with destroyed heart!

*^♠🏛♠^*

Successfully he showed them all,
That with love they can rise above,
This done once more with happy joy,
He returned to that Heaven of Love!

Comment
This is my thoughts because I believe the soul leaves the body at the time of death... and that no way was our Lords Soul imprisoned in the tomb for 3 days along with his body and that he returned to show us this the truth with love!

*^♠🏛♠^**^♠🏛♠^**^♠🏛♠^*

ﺷﺷ♣ﺷﺷ⟰ﺷﺷ♣ﺷﺷ

The Winners Bow

When hearts love all men will we see?
Heaven on Earth for you and me,
I'm afraid not unless we change our ways,
By ensuring we have some tomorrow days!

*^♠⟰♠^*

The trees on Earth were given by God,
By stripping Earth of them we're making a rod,
One that will whip us and show much pain,
When the forests no longer help produce rain!

*^♠⟰♠^*

With no roots for earth to grip on I warn,
We'll see more sand like a dessert storm!
The air to will be full of poisonous gas,
So these things we must not let come to pass!

*^♠⟰♠^*

The worst and most important war we must win,
Is what man does to Earth, being the biggest sin!
This is a war we must be ready to fight,
We must stop greed taking a bite!

*^♠⟰♠^*

We must all be prepared to take a cut,
Stop stripping away, but replace and put,
Back, replant, replace, restore,
Go back to living by nature's law!

*^♠⟰♠^*

It still won't be Heaven if all men love,
If the Earth is stripped and air poisoned above!
We have to start showing some loving care now,
So one day man can take the winners bow!

*^♠⟰♠^**^♠⟰♠^**^♠⟰♠^*

Don't Feel Guilty

Feeling guilty is a normal reaction for all,
That cares when a loved one as taken a fall
We all do this when a loved one has gone,
Wishing there was more that we had done.

*^♠⛪♠^*

This is all a part of grieving because we love,
Missing the one who has gone above,
We all could have done more that is true,
By another deed, or by talking things through!

*^♠⛪♠^*

But we're only human after all's said and done
So while we do not deliberately hurt anyone,
That we're not perfect we must accept the fact,
And learn from it if we failed to act!

*^♠⛪♠^*

We all do it and it's a waste of emotion,
Feeling guilty doesn't show that we had devotion,
If you loved truly the one gone will have known,
Without doing more to make feelings shown.

*^♠⛪♠^*

The loved one gone won't want to look down on you,
To see you tearing your heart and soul in two,
So if you are guilty of something then some how,
Think what they would say to you right now.

*^♠⛪♠^*

ش♣شد🏠شد♣شش

If you can't think what they'd say think what you'd do
If you'd past over to see your loved ones blue,
Crying because of what they hadn't done or said.
Wouldn't you say "Don't you worry your pretty head
*^♠🏠♠^*

Dry those tears, don't make yourself ill over me
If you love me then let it be a smile I see,
Don't waste your energies on being negative,
Fill your mind with thoughts that are positive."

*^♠🏠♠^*

So although it's normal to fee this guilt,
Remember no future can ever be built,
On something that is as destructive as this,
Better to just say goodbye and blow them a kiss!

Knowing that the physical things you didn't do,
Can wait till the day that you go through,
That delicate thin veil that keeps you apart,
Till then just speak of what's in your heart.

LOVE.

If You Feel Guilty It's Only Because You Loved
And You cared So Stop it!

*^♠🏠♠^**^♠🏠♠^**^♠🏠♠^*

Marianthi Birch

My loving caring friend who tries to help in all you do,
A true believer in God's love, a peace creator like a dove!
Raising her voice only to give, praise to others as they live!
Inspiring all who come near to trust in God without fear
A healer a giver a creator of hope, showing others how to cope
Nurturing love wherever she goes, truly proving that it flows!
Teaching others how to pray to send out healing everyday!
Her love inspired a group to pray together in a healing way!
In this she's an Angel true, within the Gard-Angels I tell you!

Being so constant with her love for all on earth and God above
Investing time, showing care, sending healing out in prayer!
Remembering all never thinking self knowing her is my wealth
Christ will find joy in such as she, seeing His love come to be!
Honoured deeply in heart and soul where loving all is the goal!

This you see in my friend all the time, I had the honour of helping her found a healing prayer group in the South of France, which we named The Gard-Angels...Because we all live in the Gard/Provence Region...
Bless you Marianthi you are a true sister full of Christ's Love.

*^♠♟♠^**^♠♟♠^**^♠♟♠^*

ﺷﺷ▓ﺷ▓ﺷﺷ🏛ﺷ▓ﺷ▓ﺷﺷ

A Gard Angel Has Risen

One of the Gard-Angels has taken flight,
Helen, to be in God's arms tonight!
In Heaven where she inspired to go,
Because she loved Our Dear Lord so!
Yes! A member's gone from our group,
One we'll find hard to recoup!
One who gave out such loving care,
Only thinking of others in healing prayer!
Our Helen now we won't meet with a kiss
On Thursdays when her face we'll miss!
But we know she'll be listening up above,
Sending out healing to all we love!
Helen! We know will still help us to heal,
That her presence we'll still feel!
For with her risen now to Heaven above,
We've a real true Angel healing with love!

*^♠♟♠^*

The Gard-Angels are a healing group in the South of France so called because
they are based in the lovely Gard Region, Helen joined us at the very
beginning and she was always a big pillow of strength for all
GOD BLESS YOU HELEN
We will miss you, though we know you will always be near!
*^♠♟♠^**^♠♟♠^**^♠♟♠^*

153

ش‍ش‍ش‍ش‍ش‍ش‍ش‍ش‍ش

Playing in the Parks a Lark

With loving joy I watched other kids play,
Then went over to them so I could say!
"Will you let me to join in with you?
For I'd love to do the things you do"

They said, "Yes!" So together we all did skip,
Although very often in the rope I'd trip!
But nobody cared they just smiled and carried on,
Singing songs as we jumped having fun!

Then after we all ran to the seesaw,
Having a go in turn with either three or four.
Riding on the seesaw while the others sat,
Till along came Johnnie saying enough of that!

*^♠⬆♠^*

How about we play a game or two,
Of football because there's enough of you.
So we did and played five a side,
I was goalie and saved them with pride!

*^♠⏰♠^*

Then game over, we all went home to bed,
Each one like me with a sleepy head!
Worn out with playing in real fresh air,
Running and laughing without a care!

*^♠⏰♠^*

I went to sleep thinking I can't wait till tomorrow,
When I can play again, but then with sorrow!
I woke up to find it was all a dream I'd had,
Playing out with the kids being glad!

*^♠⏰♠^*

Then I looked at my play station with latest game,
Thinking its ok! But not really the same!
As playing outside and having a lark,
With all other kids out in the park!

Comment
I think it a real shame that children today
do not have the freedom to go out and play,
that the only games they know are mostly
played on a screen.

*^♠⏰♠^**^♠⏰♠^**^♠⏰♠^*

155

Let's

Let's go clip away the old wood,
So we can flourish and grow,
Why wait until a bad wind,
Comes to do it with a blow!

*^♠🏠♠^*

Let's get rid of all the clutter,
That keeps us hemmed in,
Without space to move,
So all we do is spin!

*^♠🏠♠^*

Let's do away with uncertainty,
Of not knowing about tomorrow,
By making sure each new day,
Is a better one to follow!

*^♠🏠♠^*

Let's be like nature in winter,
Have a good clear out so we,
Get rid of all the deadwood
For a spring in our step to see!

*^♠🏠♠^*

Let's stop hanging on to daydreams,
That we know will never come true,
Far better we let HOPE guide us,
To a positive outlook anew!

*^♠🏠♠^**^♠🏠♠^**^♠🏠♠^*

The Lad I Married

Always been there, through every day,

Never missing a chance, to come and play.

Throughout childhood you were always there,

Helping to make the memories we share,

Oh! What great times we had as kids together,

Nothing's spoilt it, not even the weather,

You and I married on re-bound too young, they said!

(48 years ago)

Seems we certainly did prove them all wrong,

It helped that we both sang the same song,

Music and laughter always helped us through,

Past all heartaches that came to make us blue,

Still together in our autumn years,

Openly expressing our laughter and tears,

Not running like we did when young kids at play,

(But gently strolling towards sunset every day)

*^♠♟♠^**^♠♟♠^**^♠♟♠^*

A Pyramid of Light

A

True Prayer
Said from Your heart!
Helps others Rise over pain!
The Angels send A light projected
To heal another and Make their heart gain!
Through loving shown In a positive bright light
The healing Angels do come Down to embrace with might

All those folk spoken of to Our Father with caring emotion!
Showing how love goes round Forming circles of true devotion

All these thoughts sent out Last to return shining bright!
Say prayers for those people Ill and those grieving at night!
Caring to relate with others Gives all chance to rise above
To live with our loved one's in Heaven's paradise with love
If we join in prayer to get our Thoughts seen by Angels above

*^♠🏛♠^**^♠🏛♠^**^♠🏛♠^*

شد۩شد۩شد۩شد

A Deed A Day

A deed a day helps you on life's way,
By lighting a cell in your soul,
So trying to light one everyday,
Should really be your goal!

For the soul is a living energy,
That gets lighter when you light a cell,
Each cell as its own little shiny light,
That vibrates when lit like a bell!

Now any cell can be easily lit,
By any good deed that you do,
For each deed creates the spark,
To light another cell in you!

Good deeds are not hard to do,
Sometimes it only takes a smile,
Or a firm shoulder to lean on,
For that someone in need, a while!

The more cells you light throughout life,
The brighter and lighter your soul will be,
So that when your time comes to depart,
You'll join the light to rise above easily!

*^♠♙♠^**^♠♙♠^**^♠♙♠^*

ﺷـﻪﺷـﺪﺷـﻪﺷﺸﺪ

Why God?

Oh! God there is so much beauty I see,
So why can't I see any in me?

Oh! God when I look at your creation,
Why do I feel such desolation!

All the beauty you created with pride,
Why isn't there any in my inside!

Why can't I feel as well as see?
All the beauty surrounding me!

Why doesn't it soak in every pore?
So I feel beauty in my core!

Please God let the beauty of your love,
Help me to rise up above,

Out of the depths of self destruction,
Please! Let me see a big reduction,

In the thoughts that destroy self worth,
To give new confidence a birth!

So that when I look at the beauty around,
I know there's some inside me found!

Then once it's within me let it flow,
Out to touch all I know!

*^♠♤^**^♠♤^**^♠♤^*

ﺷﺪﷺﺷﺪ♣ﺷﺪﷺﺷﺪ♣ﺷﺪ

How Great Thou Art

Healing with a loving touch,

On a word of prayer,

Without any hands we feel much!

Giver of life,

Redeemer of soul,

Enduring through all our strife,

A comforter that lets us see,

There is always life!

Through eyes shut or blinded,

He gives the vision to see,

Open armed he holds us,

Universally!

Always helping if we fall,

Rejoicing once we hear the call,

To rise above to loved one's all!

*^♠♟♠^**^♠♟♠^**^♠♟♠^*

شد شدๆشด🏛شدๆشد

At One with God

As I go up the mountain on hairpin bends high,
Through rocky terrain where trees reach the sky,
Sunlight through leaves makes a flickering sight,
Highlighting the picture that gives delight!

I take deep breaths to fill my lungs and heart,
With fresh mountain air letting stale depart,
Once done I feel that I'm part of the scene,
At one with God on the mountain green!

*^♠🏛♠^*

As I hear birds sing I know they rejoice,
Like me thanking God in beautiful voice,
Each twitter of song is a Thank you! I know,
To God for the beautiful nature on show!

*^♠🏛♠^*

شد♣شد🏠شد♣شد

How I wish I could sing in a voice so sweet,
To Thank the Lord for my Tony's heart beat,
For my prayers were answered healing is seen,
So together we'll stand on the mountain green!

*^♠🏠♠^*

Yes! As soon as he's fit and able to walk,
We'll come on this mountainside to talk
To God like the birds to say Thank You"
For being there again to pull us through!

*^♠🏠♠^*

Oh! It may be a trek to get up there high,
But once on the mountain we feel a part of the sky,
At one with Our Father in heaven above,
Where everyone sings in rejoicing love!

Then on that mountainside as we breathe in the air,
And look at the beauty God created with care,
We'll see his light shining through trees in sunrays
And we'll cherish his love for the rest of our days!

*^♠🏠♠^**^♠🏠♠^**^♠🏠♠^*

Secrets of Togetherness

Happy 48 Years!
Tony & Pat

Play together	Talk together,
School together	Walk together,
Love together	Flow together,
Meld together	Grow together,
Plan together	Scheme together,
Rise together	Dream together!
Fret together	Sigh together,
Cope together	Cry together!
Smile together	Laugh together,
Wear together	Graft Together!
Hope together	Question together,
Pray together	STAY TOGETHER*!*

*^♠♠^**^♠♠^**^♠♠^*

164

The Pendulum Swings

Forty-eight years now we have been wed,
Many congratulations we heard said,
All the good wishes that were sent our way,
We will cherish like we do every day!
We've had our ups and we've had our downs,
We've had much laughter and some frowns,
But we've been blessed to know loyalty,
And true friendship for all to see!
Since babes we've always played together,
Out on the backs outside in any weather,
Under the lamp down the row,
Where older kids kept the young in tow!
Looking back I don't remember a day,
When Tony wasn't there with us at play,
He'd call for my brother Wilf each day,
But he's not coming till he's done pots I would say!
Yes! My brother Wilf was Tony's play mate,
The we got wed and that changed his fate!
For it was bachelor Wilf doing the calling now,
To invite Tony out for a pint at the Plough!
Then I'd tell Tony like I told our Wilf before,
He's to do the chores before he goes out the door
, He'll wash these pots and peel the spuds too
Before he's off gallivanting with you!
Then just as Tony helped Wilf now Wilf helped too,
With the chores getting done far quicker by two!
We're still good pals and we laugh today,
About the pendulum swinging Tony's way!

شـ♣ششدⵧشـ♣ششد

'Let All See The Light

Dear God let your loving light today,
Beam down on all for whom we pray,
No matter how far away they are,
Let your light touch them from afar!

*^♠⚑♠^*

The sick the weak the young and old,
Those with nothing and those lost in gold!
Let them find you for the healing they need,
The cure for sickness and all the greed!

*^♠⚑♠^*

Let your loving light let everyone see,
How much better of they would be,
If they never strayed from out its beam,
That peace for all would be more than a dream!

*^♠⚑♠^*

ششـ♣شـ♠شـ♟شـ♣شـشش

So Father God Let your loving light,
Beam on all each and every night,
We need your light Lord to show the way,
As we walk along our life's pathway!

*^♠♟♠^*

Light the pathway Lord that leads to you,
So we can climb out potholes we fall into,
Especially those who are most in need,
Let your healing light grab them at speed!

*^♠♟♠^*

To touch their hearts to lighten their soul,
To help them take on a worthy role,
A role in life as a leader to show,
The next generation the way to go!

*^♠♟♠^*

Dear Lord let your light shine in every window,
To touch all inside and give them a glow,
Of lasting family love that will grow not wilt,
Because YOU are the foundation on which they built!

*^♠♟♠^**^♠♟♠^**^♠♟♠^*

شد♣شد♣شد🏛شد♣ششد

Other Books by This Author

Highly Recommended wonderful spiritual books and delightful
story/Poetry books for children
Read all about them at Pat's Website

www.patthepoet.com

More of Pat's books

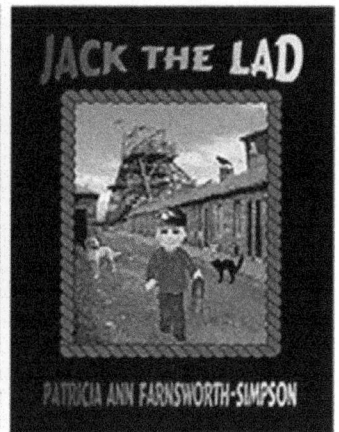

Yes! Pat is a much published Author that delights in writing poems about God and His Love as well as her great love of writing children's books full of Pat told over the years to her grandchildren...
Pat says, "These stories all tell wonderful, magical adventure stories that will delight and enthral both girls and boys, commanding their interest so that they learn the art and enjoyment of reading, as well as learning the moral that each story portrays...full with delightful pictures to enhance these make a great collection...

To purchase Pat's Books go to the publishers

Passion for Poetry

www.pfppublishers.com

شـ🍀شـ🍀شـ⛪شـ🍀ششـ

Passion for Poetry Authors/Books

Tales of a Tiny Dog

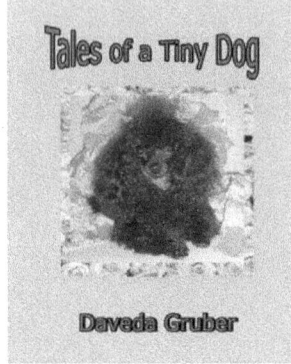

This book is in full color and has pictures of people and dogs that are a part of Daveda's enchanting life. Give the child in your life a real treat. Let them read and see the tales of a tiny dog name Lady Godiva. She is a chocolate teacup poodle that weighs four pounds, full grown; a small but mighty pup that will win many a heart! By Daveda Gruber

More Snapshots

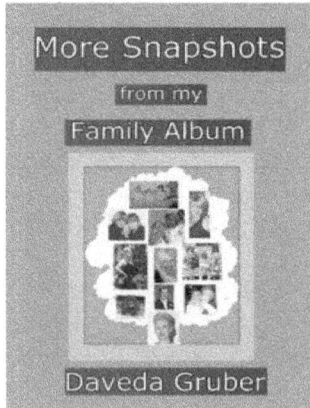

This book is Daveda Gruber's follow up to "Snapshots ...a Blonde View". Daveda is a storyteller who can tell a story to rhyme that will capture the interest of anyone! Daveda takes you on a lighthearted journey from childhood to becoming a wife, sister, mother and friend. Come along, but hold on tight when you join Daveda, as she journeys through a unique life that is all her own!

For more details on these books/ Author visit
www.pfppublishers.com

ش♣شد♪شⒸشↂ♣ششد

Amazing Pets & Animals

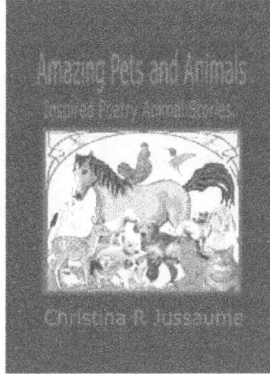

This collection of poetry was inspired by all the loving pets I have had and still have. It is poetry stories of all the many different memories we did share together in love and harmony. I also have included some fantasy story poems about animals that both adults and children will enjoy. There are some fables within this collection with a moral that teaches values. I have also created a few new invented poetry styles. All of my poetry is inspired by God, my life and inspiration from my family and pets. By Christina R Jussaume.

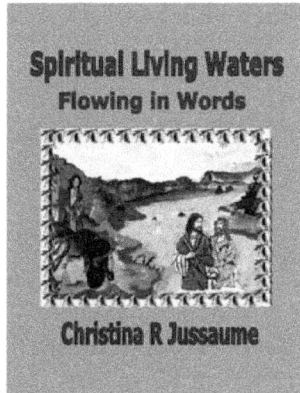

This is a book of God inspired poetry written to inspire and help others that have trials to face in life! Here you will find poetic words of love and wisdom portrayed in various ways to give comfort and peace, It is a most wonderful spiritual God loving book with many lovely pictures throughout the pages. Poets reading will truly enjoy seeing over 40 different styles of poetry displayed with a full glossary to explain each style! A book flowing with words like spiritual waters! A Must!   By Christina R Jussaume

For more details on these books/ Author visit
www.pfppublishers.com

171

Spiritual Thoughts on Love & Life

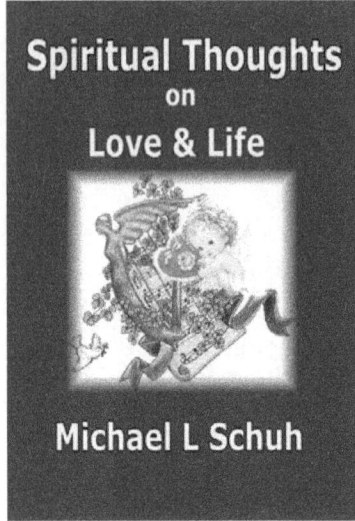

This is a wonderful poetry book full of many beautiful poems to show Mike's love of God. It is also full of many poems on love, marriage, joy and loss... Within it's pages there are many poems that all will relate too as these poems clearly portray the joy found with love, the pain found with loss and how God's love is there to support constantly. The cover designed by Pat Simpson shows the Cherub with the heart to reflect the love within and the Music, Dove and Ivy to reflect life! This book is a great collection for all who love Spiritual Poetry.
By
Michael L Schuh

For more details on these books/ Author visit
www.pfppublishers.com

ش♣ش🏛ش♣ششش
The Trojan Horse

"The Trojan Horse"
was inspired from that tragic September 11th.
He is now living in Nashville where he resides with his
Family and continues writing poetry, acting and some
Amateur painting! Erich's poetry is written for
All ages to enjoy, and he hopes it will take you on
A Pleasant Journey!
By
Erich j Goller

For more details on these books/ Author visit
www.pfppublishers.com

ﺷ♣ﺷﺷ🏠ﺷ♣ﺷﺷ

The Butterbee At Play
With Kid's In The USA!

By
Poet's World wide!

A compilation of poems and short stories from poets/ authors world-wide! All contributed to produce this book which all the proceeds will go to the Save The Children... it is a wonderful collection of poems and stories that both adults and children will enjoy reading... as all are have been written to show children that with love and understanding you can overcome troubles to stand tall... anyone purchasing this book will get wonderful joy reading and also with knowing that they too have helped raise funds for the kids charity....by Poets World-Wide

The Lucky Grub Book
or
Poems & Stories to Delight

Poet's World-Wide

The Lucky Grub Book of Poems & Stories to Delight.
by Poets World-Wide
A delightful book for all children to love and read, one too that will be greatly enjoyed by all who love reading poetry with a story/message written within. This book is like taking a magical journey through life, where love of God triumphs and loving care of children, animals both pets and wild are shown within the pages. A book passionately put together by poets world-wide to give children pleasure and encourage them to read more, but also to help raise funds for sick children in need as every author taking part as donated their work and their share of royalties to this very worthy cause... The Sick Children's Hospital in Toronto!

For more details on these books/ Author visit
www.pfppublishers.com

174

شد♣شد⛪شد♣ششد

Passion For Poetry!

Contact E.Mail: p.f.p.publishers@gmail.com

www.ingramcontent.com/pod-product-compliance
Lightning Source LLC
Chambersburg PA
CBHW032101080426
42733CB00006B/362